Essential Books for Your
Magickal Library

THE WELL-READ

WITCH

By

Carl McColman

NEW PAGE BOOKS
A division of The Career Press, Inc.
Franklin Lakes, NJ

The Well-Read Witch

Edited by Kristen Mohn
Typeset by Eileen Dow Munson
Cover design by Cheryl Cohan Finbow
Printed in the U.S.A. by Book-mart Press

To order this title, please call toll-free 1-800-CAREER-1 (NJ and
Canada: 201-848-0310) to order using VISA or MasterCard, or for further information on books from Career Press.

The Career Press, Inc., 3 Tice Road, PO Box 687,
Franklin Lakes, NJ 07417
www.careerpress.com
www.newpagebooks.com

Library of Congress Cataloging-in-Publication Data

McColman, Carl.
    The well read witch : essential books for your magickal library / by Carl
McColman
        p.cm.
    Includes bibliographical references and index.
    ISBN 1-56414-530-1
    1.   Magic—Bibliography. I Title

    Z6878.M3 M33 2001
    [BF1611]
    016.1334'3—dc21

                                                        2001044395

ACKNOWLEDGMENTS

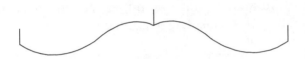

Many people have provided help, advice, support, encouragement, and (most important of all) recommendations of books to review. Thanks to Lord Athanor, Lord Dewrdrych, Nina L. Diamond, Diona, Lord Dorian, Cathryn Ellen, Judith Hawkins-Tillirson, David Herman, Lord Hermes, Gwen Knighton, Mike Lewis, Lady Magdalena, Lord Mikiel, Tom Murphy, Karen Price, Lady Ramona, Raven, Rayna, Lisa Roggow, Linda Roghaar, Pam Williams and Lord Ziggy Deucalion, and everyone at New Leaf Distributing, New Page Books, the House of Oak Spring, the Grove of the Unicorn, and the Earth Mystic Meditation Circle.

Thanks to everyone who participated in my online survey at *www.wellreadwitch.com*, or who has taken the time to develop Wiccan Web sites with recommended readings lists, or posted Wiccan booklists on *Amazon.com*. There are too many of you to list by name, but I appreciate your love of books as well as your willingness to share your opinions.

Heartfelt thanks to Dennis O'Connor, who, on a summer afternoon at Dumbarton Oaks in 1983, suggested I read Starhawk's *The Spiral Dance*. That was a decisive moment in my journey to the Goddess. *The Well-Read Witch* is my tribute to that life-changing recommendation.

Kudos to Lady Aurora Twilight, Lady Devayana Augusta, Numina, and Linda Sherer, who read early drafts of this book and offered many valuable suggestions. Special thanks to Francesca De Grandis for her thoughtful perspective on the relationship between oral tradition and the written word. Finally, my deepest thanks go to Lady Galadriel, who not only gave generously of her time by recommending books from her extensive library, but also shared her thoughts on the role of the written word in Witchcraft *and* offered her comments on an early draft of this book. Of course, the warts that remain are my responsibility.

This book is dedicated to the healing of the earth—and to everyone who has ever recommended a book they enjoy to a person they love.

Contents

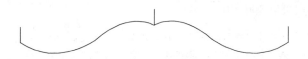

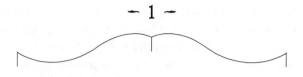

1

BELL, BOOK, AND CANDLE: THE ROLE OF THE BOOK IN WITCHCRAFT

I recently had the good fortune to be a guest at a small coven of traditional Witches in western Georgia for their Summer Solstice ritual. The High Priestess of this group—a good friend and business associate of mine—had impressed me with her depth of knowledge and balanced perspective concerning the old religion. Like many traditionalists, she and her coven prefer to keep to themselves, so when the unusual offer to join in their rites came, I did not hesitate to accept.

As it turned out, there were seven of us present that evening, four guests and three coveners. We cast the circle, chanted the Witches' Rune, and shared cakes and wine in a serene and lovely rite. After the circle, we gathered in the kitchen for a simple feast of salads, breads, and cold cuts. As we stood around the kitchen table fixing our sandwiches, I brought up one of my favorite subjects: books.

I asked the group, "What was the first book you read when you initially became interested in Witchcraft?" Among the seven of us were elders who had practiced the old ways for over 20 years, as well as students who had been in the Craft only a year or two. As I suspected, each person had a different answer. One of the students spoke first. "Well, my first book was Scott Cunningham's *The Truth About Witchcraft Today*." Someone else followed with "I think my first was *Magical Rites from the Crystal Well* by Ed Fitch."

Around the table we went. Among the books mentioned were Sybil Leek's *Diary of a Witch*, Raymond Buckland's *Complete Book of Witchcraft*, Gerald Gardner's *The Meaning of Witchcraft*, and Leo Martello's *Witchcraft, the Old Religion*. Finally I revealed my first book, Starhawk's *The Spiral Dance*.

From there, the conversation veered off into a friendly, if spirited, discussion of the merits (and failings) of each of these books. We were a boisterous group, and no one lacked a point of view. At one point someone said, "Gather three Witches together and you'll have five opinions on a topic." This certainly seemed true about the books we were discussing. We all agreed on one thing, however: each of us, from the newest student to the most veteran third-degree initiate, had first answered the call of the Goddess by reading a book. We may have had strong (and differing) opinions about the books we hold in high regard, but without exception, we were all readers.

"Here, read this book."

Most people's first encounter with Witchcraft comes through the written word. Also known as Wicca, the old religion, or simply the Craft, Witchcraft has enjoyed a major revival in the past 50 years. The resurgence of Wicca is a central part of the rebirth of Pagan (or Neopagan) spirituality—the spirituality of Nature. This revival is due, in no small part, to the many books that have been published on this spiritual path.

Indeed, a written description for a workshop presented by Wiccan author Phyllis Curott at the 2001 Pagan Spirit Gathering flatly described the Pagan community as "largely self-taught from books." Although the call to practice Nature spirituality comes ultimately from the Goddess, for many people that call initially arrives through words on a page (or screen). Up until the mid-1990s, the easiest way for most people to learn about Wicca involved reading a book or two on the subject. More recent newcomers to the Craft are as likely to use the Internet as their portal of entry, but even when it is gussied up by a graphics-rich Web site, the written word is still the written word.

The reason for this is simple. Even in our increasingly tolerant age, most Wiccans stay "in the broomcloset" about their spirituality. Unfortunately, tolerance toward Witches remains in short supply, even now in the 21st century. Teachers have lost their jobs and parents have lost custody of their children, thanks to the ongoing fear and misunderstanding about the old religion. So, except for the still relatively uncommon situations where children grow up in a Wiccan family or trusting friends confide in one another, for the most part, those who feel drawn to Wicca will find their initial contact with the old religion through words on a page.

This was certainly true for me. I first heard about Wicca through rumors and hearsay that floated around my college campus in the late 70s and early 80s. At one point, the religion department offered a class on Paganism and the Occult. The class filled before I could register for it, but one of my best friends did enroll and told me what she learned. The professor praised Witchcraft as a benevolent, earth-based system of natural healing, herbalism, and seasonal rituals and celebrations. Furthermore, he said it was a living tradition, still practiced although mostly in secret. I soon learned how true this was: shortly thereafter, my girlfriend (but not I) received an invitation to a full moon ritual held by a coven of Dianic Witches that barred men from participating in their rites. Not only was the ritual hidden from me by virtue of my gender, but it was hidden from just about everyone: only invited guests received directions to the remote rural site where the ritual took place.

Obviously, I could not learn about Wicca through classes my friends took or rumors of secret rituals. But before long the topic came up again. During a conversation on alternative forms of spirituality with an old friend, he suggested that I read a book on Wicca—*The Spiral Dance* by Starhawk.

Ah. There was the missing link. If I couldn't find an introductory seminar on the Craft advertised in my local paper, at least I could devour a book on the topic. I promptly went out and found a copy of Starhawk's book, and reading it literally changed my life.

I didn't become a Wiccan immediately after reading *The Spiral Dance*. Actually, I was quite cautious about Goddess spirituality, thanks to a conservative Southern upbringing; indeed, years would pass before I would participate in a Craft ritual or formally embrace Nature spirituality as my chosen path. But my long and involved process of discovering the old religion mirrored what many people go through, even if they don't take as long as I did. First, I read books—plenty of them. I read books by Starhawk, Margot Adler, Janet and Stewart Farrar, Raymond Buckland, and others. Eventually, I started doing rituals on my own. And finally, I began to participate in communal Pagan rites and sought out a Wiccan elder to teach me all that can never be transmitted through books. I now know that, without taking the time to read the books and learn enough about the Craft so that I felt safe and comfortable with it, I might never have embraced the ways of the Goddess.

Granted, I was more hesitant than many would-be Wiccans. For lots of folks, reading just one book is all it takes before they're looking for a coven or trying out the basic rituals of solitary Witchcraft. But even when one book is all it takes for a person to choose the old religion as their spiritual path, years after their initiation or dedication to the Goddess, such folks will look back and acknowledge how that first book played a pivotal role in their spiritual development.

The pen is mightier than the sword, or so the proverb goes. I believe the growth of modern Wicca demonstrates just how mighty words can be. Monotheistic religions like Christianity and Islam spread because of aggressive, often violent, policies of forced conversion. Wicca, on the other hand, actually opposes the practice of converting others—but even without trying, Witchcraft has emerged as one of the fastest growing religions of our time. Goddess and Nature spirituality speak beautifully to the spiritual yearnings and longings of so many people living today. But the Craft's rapid growth is due in no small part to the power of the written word. A generation of authors have presented Wicca in a way that speaks to the spiritual needs of thousands of people—who have responded by embracing this path as their own.

Turning over a New Leaf

In 1997, I landed what many Pagans would regard as a dream job: I became a buyer for the New Leaf Distributing Company, the world's largest wholesaler of metaphysical products. As such, I gained access to a warehouse filled with tens of thousands of spiritual, mystical, occult, and Wiccan books—what one of my co-workers affectionately described as "the modern equivalent to the library of Alexandria." Almost every day when my shift ended I would be poring over the extensive inventory of books on every imaginable Mind/Body/Spirit topic. New Leaf carried hundreds of books on Witchcraft and Paganism alone. With few exceptions, if it was in print, New Leaf had it.

Soon my personal library of books on the Craft—as well as on numerous other esoteric topics—began to swell. Before long, I began to wonder how to pick the books most worth reading. There weren't enough hours in the day to read all the books available on the old religion; furthermore, I soon began to see how some books were better than others. Occasionally I would run into a book filled with silly or erroneous information—for example, one author insisted that in ancient times Celtic Pagans used pumpkins in their Samhain rites, even though the pumpkin is from the New World and wouldn't have made it to Europe until the modern era.

With so many books available on Wicca, how does someone figure out the best books to read? In asking that question, I got the idea to write *The Well-Read Witch*. I knew I would have liked a guidebook to help me find some of the better books that are available—especially ones that may not be bestsellers. Perhaps anyone who wanted to become well-read, or thoroughly knowledgeable, on the subject of Witchcraft would hopefully find such a guidebook useful.

Something else I noticed in my exploration of the New Leaf warehouse: most, in fact nearly all, books about Wicca are written for beginners. Indeed, many of the books seemed to simply recycle the same basic material. How many times does someone need to be told that south represents the Element Fire and west represents Water? Granted, different books explored Wicca from the perspective of different traditions, or different points of view—Starhawk wrote about Wicca as a California feminist and a political activist, while Sybil Leek wrote about the Craft from a much more conservative, traditional, British perspective. And therein lay another important point: Wicca is big enough for people with many different political or social views. It is not just a religion for feminists or environmentalists (even though such groups are certainly well represented in the Craft community). Furthermore, I realized that if a conservative person first encountered Wicca through the writings of Starhawk, he or she might be turned off and never give Wicca another chance. Likewise, an ardent feminist might find Leek's traditionalist position to be distasteful. So I realized that the various books for beginners were meant for a wide variety of people—and Goddess help them to find the book that would actually speak to them.

And what about the non-beginners? Well, Starhawk had written a few books about Wicca from the feminist perspective, and there were a couple of books that dealt with issues related to running a coven or leading rituals. A few academically-oriented books were available, usually published by University presses in expensive hardback editions. But other than that, little seemed to exist. What was the intermediate or advanced Wiccan to read? Of course, much Wiccan lore is preserved exclusively in the oral tradition, and a person needs to be involved in a coven to learn such things. But the way I saw it, to be well-read on the subject of Witchcraft, a person needs more than just books for beginners.

And that's when I realized that many of the most important books in a Witch's library might not have any obvious connection to Wicca or Witchcraft at all.

It's like this: Wicca is a path of healing; therefore, Wiccans need to be familiar with various natural and spiritual healing modalities. Wicca is a path of ritual and celebration; therefore, Witches need to have a sense of mythology and ritual design. Wicca is a path of Nature reverence and worship; therefore, Wiccans would do well to have a strong understanding of life sciences and environmental issues. Witchcraft is a path of Goddess worship; therefore, it benefits Witches to know the history of such spirituality and the feminist issues associated with it. And on and on it goes.

Aha! I realized. Becoming a well-read Witch requires reading much more than just books on Witchcraft, no matter how informative or useful such books might be. The Wiccan books that I enjoyed reading and collecting were only the tip of the iceberg. To thoroughly explore the Craft, one must learn about herbalism, study magick, develop psychic skills, and practice the art of meditation—and much, much more. With this realization, the concept of *The Well-Read Witch* fell into place.

Two questions

So in writing this book, I hope to address two key questions:

First: What are excellent books on Wicca, especially for the person unfamiliar with or new to the Craft? This includes not only books for beginners, but also books for the intermediate and advanced practitioner (yes, such books do exist, and more are coming out all the time). It also would include classics from the past, many now out of print, for people who are interested in the history of modern Witchcraft.

But the second question is equally important: What books deserve to be on the lifetime reading list of people dedicated to Wicca as their primary spiritual path? What are the best books in the many areas of interest to Wiccans, such as healing, magick, ritual, and mythology?

For the second question especially, my list of books functions mainly as a teaser—an attempt to point out just a few of the many wonderful books out there. A person could read the books listed in the pages to come and develop a reasonably broad general knowledge of topics of interest to most Witches: divination, herbalism, psychic development, and so forth. Sooner or later, most people who pursue the ways of the Goddess will feel drawn to study one or more of these topics in greater depth. I had lunch recently with an astrologer friend of mine and we talked about how a person could study no other esoteric discipline besides astrology and still have a lifetime's worth of work to pursue. The same is true with the Tarot, or meditation, or Celtic mythology. So while the books listed here will help anyone to get a taste of the many different disciplines of interest to Witches, this list by no means represents all there is to know on any one topic. I offer this list of books as, hopefully, a good start.

2

BOOK OF SHADOWS: ORAL TRADITION AND THE WRITTEN WORD

Do all these books on Witchcraft (and related subjects) make the traditional way of learning Wicca—through studying with a coven or a Craft elder—no longer necessary?

If you want to follow the old ways, an important part of your spiritual path will consist of reading up on the Craft and related subjects. But it takes more than reading books to become a Witch. In the words of Lady Galadriel, a Wiccan elder of the Unicorn tradition and editor of *The New Wiccan Book of the Law*, "Books may reveal the *secrets* of Witchcraft. But they cannot ever reveal the *mysteries*. A mystery can only be experienced." To become a Witch requires both knowledge of Wiccan secrets and the direct experience of Wiccan mysteries.

Look at it this way: If a person read *The Joy of Sex* and any number of other books on sexuality but had never felt the pounding of two hearts while kissing and embracing a loved one, could that person truly be called an accomplished lover?

Of course not. The books may provide all sorts of erotic knowledge, but without the experience of actually making love, a person remains a virgin. Of course, there's nothing wrong with being a virgin. But until someone experiences the beauty of love, reading all the sex books in the world is nothing more than an exercise of the mind.

The same principle applies to Goddess spirituality. There are two ways to gain knowledge of the old ways, through the written word and through one or more teachers of the Craft. Anyone who is interested in Wicca will probably enjoy reading all they can on the subject and will also likely enjoy classes, especially if taught by a knowledgeable and responsible teacher. But amassing knowledge is only half of the process of embracing the Goddess. The other half comes through experience. This includes experience with ritual, meditation, vision quest, initiation, and psychic development. Of course, every person's path is unique, and what I require to become mature in my spiritual path may not be the same as what you require. Nevertheless, it takes more than just reading a book to master the Craft of the Wise.

Some people more naturally pursue the experiential side of spirituality, enjoying spellwork, trancework, and other hands-on activities. Others more naturally prefer to immerse themselves into the esoteric knowledge that can only be gained through study, whether reading books, working with a teacher, or both. Sometimes it's easy to focus on just one of these paths, the experiential or the intellectual; and often a seeker will choose one and ignore the other. So some people read tons of books but never seek out the direct experience of Pagan spirituality. Others immerse themselves in the experience, but avoid the work of book-learning.

I'd like to encourage you to seek balance here. Read all you can. But know when to put the books down and experience the wisdom of the Craft. Balance intellectual knowledge with heart-felt experience.

For some, finding this balance may require the guidance of a qualified teacher or coven (something I recommend). Others may prefer a more solitary path. Those who by choice or circumstance don't have ready access to teachers or groups may need to use exercises in books to develop their skills in meditation, visualization, ritual, and intuition, all by themselves. For some people, a powerful ritual process of initiation through a traditional coven may be a crucial turning point on their journey into Nature spirituality. Others may experience profound shifts through less formal, but still powerful, experiences such as spending several days alone in the wilderness. Whatever direction your unique path may take you, remember: There's always more to learn and more to experience. The path of Wiccan spirituality balances the quest for knowledge with the attainment of experience.

Of teachers and tradition

Traditionally, Wiccan ways were passed down orally, from mother to daughter, from teacher to student, from master to apprentice. I believe studying under the guidance of a good teacher remains the single best way to learn Witchcraft. Many Craft elders not only possess vast amounts of knowledge, but also understand how to use and apply that knowledge in the service of the Goddess and the God. The best teachers know how to perform rituals that inspire, spells that work, and magick that truly transforms. In studying with such a teacher, you will learn and experience things that no book could ever teach you.

But for a variety of reasons, not everyone has access to a good teacher. Among other things, Wicca is growing so fast that there are more students eager to learn than there are qualified teachers to train them. If you are in a position where you don't have access to a teacher, do not despair. Francesca De Grandis, a Wiccan elder of the Third Road Tradition and the author of *Be a Goddess!*, says, "A good teacher and an ardently seeking student cannot be replaced by a good book and an ardently seeking student. But, good teachers are not always available, and I will suggest a good book before a bad teacher." Even without a qualified elder to teach you, you can still take responsibility for your Wiccan education by reading and doing experiential work such as meditation and ritual. Indeed, that's why elders like De Grandis have written books; they recognize there are more willing students than they personally could ever reach. Just remember: Without a teacher, you have to be your own master. The process of learning still requires actually reading the book, taking notes, doing the exercises (many Wiccan books have numerous practical exercises to do), and doing research to answer any questions that may arise. All this, while keeping knowledge in perspective with experience as you progress along your spiritual path.

It's easy to see why so many Wiccan elders continue to advocate learning the Craft from a teacher rather than just through books. "Oral tradition is based in direct individualized feedback from elders," notes Francesca De Grandis. Lady Galadriel concurs. "Until they invent the book that can talk back and answer your questions, a teacher is irreplaceable."

Controversy

I know of Wiccan elders who do not like to recommend books to their students. They think reading books can get in the way of the more important quest for spiritual experience.

On the other hand, some Wiccan books encourage the reader to perform self-initiation rituals and to value their own intuition above tradition when it comes to walking the Wiccan path.

Therein lies a controversy. What is the proper role of the written word in a tradition that, historically, has been passed down orally? With so many books getting published on Wicca and magick, and with so many newcomers to Pagan spirituality relying on books to educate themselves, with or without a mentor, perhaps books are actually doing more harm than good? If new Pagans are not bothering to learn tradition, but are simply reading a book or two and deciding that's all it takes to be a Witch, perhaps all these books are actually undermining the very religion they supposedly are promoting. On the other hand, perhaps the explosion of books is neither good nor bad, but simply a new and different way for the secrets to be transmitted?

My purpose in pointing out this controversy is not to take sides (although I personally take a moderate position, which I will explain below). But in writing about Wiccan books, I felt that I needed to acknowledge this issue. I think it represents growing pains in the Craft community. Like I said above, there are more eager students than there are qualified teachers. Part of the reason why there are so many students is because of all the Wiccan books that have come out in the last 20 or so years. The books get people interested in the old ways, but it takes more than reading a book to become a Witch—and yet, for many people, reading a book is the only education they'll get. If some books imply that teachers aren't necessary, and some teachers suggest that books aren't necessary, where is the best path to maturity in the Craft?

Through experience. And ultimately, your experience is a personal matter between you and the Goddess and the God. Reading a book does not necessarily translate into spiritual experience. Studying with a teacher does not necessarily translate into spiritual experience, either (although a teacher has the advantage of providing personalized feedback).

I cannot resolve the tension between oral tradition and written words in this little book. But I think the best position involves honoring both books and teachers for what they do best. Books transmit knowledge efficiently and enjoyably. They're easier on the eyes than a computer screen, and work equally well whether you're in bed, on the sofa, or in an airplane.

Meanwhile, working with a qualified teacher is the best strategy for mastering the experiential side of Wicca. If you don't have access to a good teacher, you can still pursue the experiential, but it takes just as much self-discipline and dedicated effort as required when working with a teacher. Maybe even more.

So I recommend a combination of enjoying the many books on Witchcraft and related subjects, along with working with a qualified teacher, as the best way to practice Wiccan spirituality. If you don't currently have access to a good teacher, perhaps in the future that opportunity will arise. Meanwhile, keep reading—and doing experiential work, like meditation and ritual. Seek knowledge of the secrets and experience of the mysteries. That is the path to becoming a Witch.

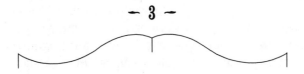

3

DISCERNMENT: HOW TO FIGURE OUT WHICH WITCH BOOKS TO READ (AND WHICH ONES TO IGNORE)

As a spiritual path, Wicca fosters a genuine climate of intellectual liberty. Witches honor and respect one another's freedom, which includes the fundamental freedom to choose what you want to read. There will never be a Wiccan equivalent to the notorious list of forbidden books put out by the Roman Catholic Church. In the Craft, nobody has any authority to forbid books. Wiccan authors do not need to get anybody's approval to write and publish their books; and neither does anyone need to get approval to read whatever they choose.

Indeed, the only force that influences the availability of Pagan or Wiccan books is sheer economics. Publishers will only bring out books they believe will make a profit; and if a book doesn't sell many copies (or its sales have dropped to a negligible amount), it will be taken out of print. Books are published not according to how good or true or useful they are, but simply by how much money they will potentially make. A brilliant book on an obscure topic that probably won't sell very many copies may never get published, whereas a schlocky book about the sex lives of Hollywood celebrities will likely be rushed to press with the author making big bucks. In commercial publishing, money makes the rules. This is not without its problems, but it's better than living in a situation where "the authorities" get to choose what we may or may not read.

Thankfully, Witchcraft has no Grand Poo-bah to decree what is worth reading (and what's not). Therefore, Witches must take responsibility for themselves in figuring out what to read. And just because a book is a bestseller doesn't automatically make it an essential book.

Wiccans, let it be known, tend to be opinionated people. From neophytes to elders, most will have definite opinions regarding the merits of this or that book. Most Witches enthusiastically recommend some books while refusing to endorse others. Although Witches usually oppose censorship, they will still acknowledge that differences in quality exist in books—like everything else.

Shortly after I began the research for this book, I realized there was no way I could ever create a single, definitive, absolute list of must-read Witch books. In a way, it would be easier to draw up a list of recommended Catholic books, since the Catholic Church has relatively specific standards of what is or isn't acceptable. But no such official standards exist in the Craft (thank the Goddess). My research involved not only reading and reviewing hundreds of books, but also soliciting the recommendations of Wiccan elders (whose opinions often conflicted), conducting an online survey, researching various coven reading lists on the Internet, and then ultimately making my own choice over which books to recommend—and which ones to leave off the list. Here's my disclaimer: *My opinions are just that—my opinions—and carry no more, nor less, weight than anyone else's.*

My goal has been to identify those titles that I believe represent the highest quality of Wiccan and spiritual writing. Incidentally, just because a book hasn't been listed here does not necessarily mean it's not a good book. Many valuable and useful books on Wicca and related topics simply didn't make the final cut.

The good, the bad, and the ugly

Why am I even raising this issue? Why don't I just publish my list of books I deem essential, and leave it at that, without making a fuss over books I *don't* recommend? There are two reasons. First, every Wiccan who talks to other Witches, even just over the Internet, will quickly run across people who hold strong opinions about this or that book. "It sucks!" "It's not *real* Witchcraft!" "The spells in it are bogus!" are some of the more common attacks leveled at books. More sophisticated critics will attack a book because of poor scholarship; because of its lack of original ideas; or because it contains sexist, racist, or homophobic material. Which leads me to my second reason for raising the quality issue. The simple fact is, some books of inferior quality do make it to print.

In the Summer 1998 issue of *Gnosis* magazine, Joanna Hautin-Mayer's article "When is a Celt not a Celt?" demonstrated how some books written for the Wiccan and Pagan community do not always meet the highest standards of scholarship. In the article, the author points out how one bestselling book on Wiccan spirituality is actually filled with historical inaccuracies; such as suggesting that potatoes were native to Ireland (the potato comes from the New World and never made it to Europe until modern times) and that Stonehenge is located in Cornwall (it's actually in Wiltshire). No book, author, or editor is perfect—but these kinds of blatant errors not only confuse people who don't know any better, but they make Wicca look bad to those who do.

Sadly, because the primary reason a book gets published is its potential to make money, some publishers seem too willing, either out of cynicism or negligence, to release books which seem destined to sell well but are poorly written, plagiarized, filled with grammatical or factual errors, or which include offensive material. Of course, most editors and publishers are scrupulously honest and committed not only to making money but also to publishing quality books. But some others may not be so ethical. The bottom line: Every person who reads books on Wicca (or indeed, on any topic) must take responsibility to determine the merits of each book. This is a tricky matter. After all, most of us read books to learn, which means we're reading about a subject that is unfamiliar to us. So how do we know if the book is a quality product or not?

There are several ways to approach this question.

Read reviews and get recommendations from people you trust. It always makes sense to see what other people think of a book or an author. If someone criticizes a book, get clear reasons why they don't like it.

When reading something, keep your own intuition alert. Always read a book with an open mind—which means you're open to questioning it (even if you like it). And look for the following warning signs. These are some questions to help you decide if a book is not for you.

- Does the book contain racist, sexist, homophobic, or other hateful/hostile messages?
- Is the tone of the book arrogant?
- Does the book take an extreme position, while heaping harsh, judgmental, or overly vicious criticism on those who disagree?
- Does the book include information you know for a fact is wrong?
- Does the book make grandiose claims, without backing them up?

- Does the book advocate any kind of negative or unloving behavior, or actions aimed at desecrating the holy symbols of other religions?

- Does the book suggest that magick involves making deals or pacts with spirits or demons, or that magick involves controlling spiritual entities?

- Does the book advocate manipulating the free will of others, or using the belongings of others (like a lock of hair) in ritual without their permission?

I began this chapter by praising the intellectual freedom within Wicca, and I want to end on that same positive note. Just because a few books get published that contain mediocre, useless, or even harmful material, doesn't mean we should have censorship or book burnings. The Quakers said it best, with their old saying, "It's better to light a candle than to curse the darkness." Fortunately, so many wonderful, beautifully written, and truly magickal books exist on Wicca and related subjects, that we really don't need to waste much time worrying about the few losers. If a book gets slammed by a critic you trust for containing sloppy scholarship or questionable ethics, simply skip over it and move on—there's sure to be a worthwhile book on the same topic. Ultimately, it will be the Wiccan community as a whole that decides what are the truly essential books, and that's a process I trust far more than anything a centralized authority could ever do. As a reader, it is your responsibility to take a part in this process of discerning what truly has the most value. So read with an open but discerning mind, and don't be afraid to discuss your opinions with others—or to learn from elders who have knowledge to share.

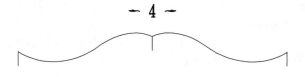

How to Use
This Book

The Well-Read Witch is designed primarily for three kinds of people:

-  The person who does not necessarily practice Wiccan or Pagan spirituality, but would like to learn more about it.

- The person new to Witchcraft who wants to learn the basics.

- The veteran Witch, who may know the basics but wants to become knowledgeable about topics that appeal to most Wiccans, such as herbalism, psychic development, or mythology.

The actual booklist begins with Chapter 6 and consists of three parts. Part One (Chapters 6-10) covers introductory, intermediate, and advanced Wiccan books, as well as Pagan books and Wiccan classics. Part Two (Chapters 11-26) explores specific elements of Wicca in greater depth, including magick, healing, herbalism, psychic development, and Wiccan views of the Goddess and the God. Part Three (Chapters 27-37) explores ways in which Wicca relates to the worlds of politics, psychology, sociology, and the arts.

For the curious onlooker or the Wiccan beginner, I recommend starting with Part One; people with more experience in the Wiccan community will probably find Parts Two and Three to be of the greatest immediate value.

Here's another way to approach the book list: Part One recommends books that will help you learn about Wicca and Paganism. Part Two recommends books that will help you develop a more in-depth knowledge of different aspects of Wiccan spirituality. Finally, Part Three recommends books that will help you understand Wicca in the larger context of living today.

Well-read Witches read more than just Witch books

Because the goal of this book is not only to help a person to become well-read about Witchcraft, but also to help Witches to become well-read in general, not all of the books profiled in Parts Two and Three are necessarily Wiccan titles. Indeed, many of the titles profiled in those sections, like Paramahansa Yogananda's *Autobiography of a Yogi* or Edgar Cayce's *Auras: An Essay on the Meaning of Colors*, do not have anything to do with Wicca at all—at least, not on the surface. Yogananda and Cayce, for example, were adherents of Hinduism and Christianity, respectively. Reading these books may not teach you anything about Wicca, but they are included because they contain material that a Wiccan may find useful in practicing Nature spirituality.

Many Wiccans want to practice a purely Pagan form of spirituality; they do not want to mix elements of Christianity or any other non-Pagan religion in with the Craft. I understand and respect such efforts and I recognize that my decision to include books from non-Pagan spiritual traditions may be upsetting to some. While I support all good-willed efforts to create a uniquely Wiccan/Pagan culture, I personally enjoy how learning of the wisdom and knowledge from many different traditions and cultures can help me grow and develop in my own. Just because I read a Buddhist book does not make me less of a Pagan, any more than reading a book about women makes me less of a man. I believe that, no matter what spiritual tradition you may follow, remaining respectfully open to the deep and authentic wisdom of other paths can actually help you to be more deeply attuned to your own path. The more secure a person is in his or her home tradition, the more he or she can learn and grow from exposure to the tremendous diversity of wisdom and knowledge found throughout the world.

One of the reasons why I felt drawn to Nature spirituality was the promise of true intellectual freedom. Unlike the monotheistic religions, Wicca and most other forms of Paganism have no dogma to restrict what one may or may not believe—or read. Instead, to walk the Pagan path means to follow one's own conscience, and to seek out truth as found in Nature. For this reason, neither non-Pagan religion nor science nor psychology nor any other branch of human knowledge can be called the enemy of the Craft; rather, any book that helps people to grow in knowledge and understanding of life can benefit the seeker of Pagan ways.

For the beginner

Still, some readers, especially those who are new to Wicca or who wish to learn specifically about the old ways of Pagan Europe, may not want to be reading about Christian psychics or Native American mythology—at least, not now. This is understandable, for the needs of Wiccan neophytes or newly initiated Witches are certainly different from the needs of elders who have practiced the old ways for many years. Thus, if you are someone who wants to read only about Wicca, I encourage you to start at the beginning. Chapters 6, 8, and 9 exclusively list books that are Wiccan in focus, arranged for the beginner, intermediate, and advanced student, respectively. Chapter 7 lists books on Paganism, most of which look at Wicca in the larger context of modern Nature spirituality. Chapter 10 is one of my favorite lists in the book: it profiles a number of Wiccan classics. I've defined a Wiccan classic as a book on modern Witchcraft published between 1939 (when Gerald Gardner's first book, *A Goddess Arrives*, was released) and 1979 (when Starhawk's *The Spiral Dance* and Margot Adler's *Drawing Down the Moon* came out). Gardner's writings first sparked the modern Wiccan movement as a publicly visible spiritual trend; while the arrival of Starhawk's and Adler's books that marked the "graduation" of Wicca from underground Occultism to an increasingly mainstream expression of Goddess worship and Nature mysticism. In those first 40 years of modern Wicca, some wonderful (and now mostly forgotten) books were published by colorful and articulate Witch-writers such as Sybil Leek, Leo Martello, Raymond Buckland, and Doreen Valiente. Reading through these books (many of which are unfortunately out of print and difficult to find) provides the student with a detailed glimpse into the early years of modern Wicca.

Other Wiccan and Pagan books are sprinkled throughout Parts Two and Three. But for someone who wants to read only about Nature spirituality, Part One contains a wealth of titles to consider. Indeed, at the rate of a book a week, it would take over a year to read every title in Chapters 6 through 10.

Naturally, there is no right order in which to read the books profiled here. Beginners would probably benefit the most by starting with Chapter 6; beyond that, it's up to you to explore the topics that interest you the most. I've given a short introduction in each chapter describing how the topic relates to Wicca as a whole, followed by the recommended titles, with a sentence or a brief paragraph describing each book.

If everyone who picks up this book finds at least one title that they did not know previously, then I will have achieved my goal. For the purpose of this book is simple: To act as an agent for introducing people to books they will likely enjoy. For serious students of Wiccan spirituality, the books listed here can represent a lifetime of reading pleasure.

Author and title

Each book is listed by author and title. I've noted if there is a special or revised edition. In the bibliography, I've included author/title/publisher/date, but I should point out that this bibliographic information refers to the copies of these books I used in my research; copies currently available through bookstores may have been released by different publishers. Many books have been published in multiple editions over the years; or in one edition in the USA and another in Europe; or a publisher changes names and old copies of a book will say Harper & Row on the spine while new copies say Harper Collins. So if you're looking for books, either through a bookstore or online, knowing the author and title will be all it takes to find most works. If your copy is in a different edition than mine, so what? The words inside are the same, and that's what really matters.

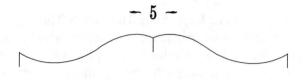

5

FOR THE BEGINNER: A BRIEF INTRODUCTION TO WICCA

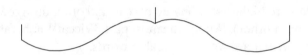

In Chapter 6, I recommend 13 books specifically written for persons with little or no knowledge of Wicca. Each of these titles provides a detailed introduction to the mystery and romance of Nature spirituality. Subsequent chapters look at intermediate and advanced Wiccan books, as well as books that cover a variety of topics that would appeal to the typical Witch.

It is not the purpose of this book to provide an in-depth explanation of Wiccan beliefs and practices for the absolute beginner. Still, I suppose some beginners will be drawn to this book, people who (like me when I first discovered Wicca) may feel safer at first just reading about Witchcraft rather than trying to meet a real Witch or finding a real coven. If this applies to you, I strongly recommend beginning with at least several of the books highlighted in Chapter 6. In the meantime, I thought it might be helpful to provide a brief overview of Witchcraft—a mysterious, wonderful, and too-often-misunderstood spiritual path.

Wicca, Witch, Pagan...

Wicca is a middle English word for Witch. The origin of the word is unclear; some writers think it means "wise" (which explains why we refer to Witchcraft as "the Craft of the Wise") while others think it means "to bend," like the bent twigs or sticks used to weave a wicker basket. This meaning suggests the magickal orientation of Wicca—for as a magickal path, Witchcraft seeks to bend or shape our lives and circumstances to promote healing, happiness, and well-being in accordance with the highest good. Some Witches do not like the word Wiccan, and some Wiccans do not like the word Witch (this is an example of one of the most basic characteristics of Wiccan culture—most Witches are highly opinionated people and often disagree even with one another). But for the most part, Wicca/Witchcraft and Wiccan/Witch are interchangeable words.

Another word often used in relation to this spiritual path is Pagan. Originally, the word Pagan meant "country-dweller," and it was kind of an insult, with a meaning similar to words like hick or country bumpkin. When the Christian religion became the dominant spiritual practice in the Roman Empire, the Pagan country folk were looked down upon by the city dwellers. The urbanites adopted the new religion, while the country bumpkins stubbornly clung to the old Gods and Goddesses. In this way, the word Pagan came to be associated with non-Christian spirituality. Nowadays, most people who consciously seek to resurrect the ancient, pre-Christian spirituality of old Europe proudly call themselves Pagans (even if they live in big cities). In a way, the country dweller meaning of Pagan still is appropriate, for most modern Pagans tend to see nature as central to their spirituality, and even if they don't actually live close to nature in a rural setting, they love and revere nature and want to have as much contact with the natural world as possible.

In order to complicate matters even further, just as not all Witches like to be called Wiccans and vice versa, so not all

Wiccans like to be called Pagans (and vice versa). Many Pagans identify more with shamanism or Druidry or Nordic spirituality than they do with Witchcraft; and therefore, many Witches regard Paganism as too broad a concept to truly explain Wicca. But there are lots of Witches and Pagans who use the two words almost interchangeably. It takes all kinds! And since I personally feel just as comfortable with the words Wiccan and Pagan as I do with Witch, I'll use all three terms more or less interchangeably. My apologies to those who disagree.

Banishing the misconceptions

What is modern Witchcraft like? To answer, let's begin by debunking some of the misconceptions. First and foremost, Wiccans do not worship the devil. In fact, Witches don't even believe the devil exists. The concept of the devil is based in the religious world-view of Christianity, which sees the cosmos like some sort of giant battlefield where the good God and the evil devil are constantly fighting. To Wiccans, the cosmos is not a battleground, but a marriage chamber. The universe is the setting where God (the Divine Masculine) and Goddess (the Divine Feminine) express their love for one another. As in any marriage, this relationship has its share of conflict, disagreement, and upset. So the love between Goddess and God does not make this world perfect. We live in a world of both light and shadow. Wiccans refuse to blame their misfortunes—or their misdeeds—on any sort of supernatural evil figure. This means that people have to take responsibility for their own actions.

Second, Wiccans do not perform black magick or cast spells designed to hurt people. The stereotype of Witches-as-evildoers is just an extension of the devil-worship myth. In truth, Wicca is based on positive qualities such as love, trust, freedom, and healing. For this reason, Wiccans practice the Craft not to hurt others, but rather to become better people themselves—more kind, more loving, more compassionate.

Granted, some people who practice Wicca may behave in harmful or destructive ways. But this is just as true of Christianity or Buddhism or any other spiritual path. Any group of people will have a few problems in the ranks. But taken as a whole, Wicca stands for positive qualities such as love, happiness, and joy. Most Wiccans want to express healing and compassion through their spiritual path.

One more misconception: Witches are not a bunch of old ugly women. Both men and women can be Witches, and Wiccan people come in all ages, shapes, and sizes. Witches can be strikingly beautiful or plain and ordinary. Witches can be slender, plump, short, tall, bony, curvaceous, and just about whatever description you can apply. In short, Wiccans look just like anyone else. And while some people who follow the Wiccan path love to dress all in black and wear lots of silver pentacles and other kind of witchy jewelry, others are perfectly happy in jeans and a sweater—or a pinstripe suit. Forget the stereotypes—most Witches can easily blend in with a crowd.

What Wicca is...

But enough of what Wicca is not. Now let's look at what Wicca is.

Wiccans love life. The Craft is not a passive spirituality of self-denial and asceticism; on the contrary, it approaches life with gusto, seeing goodness in nature and affirming that the purpose of life is to love ourselves and one another, and enjoy the pleasures of existence.

Wicca involves the modern expression of ethical Witchcraft. It is modern in that its current form dates back to about the middle of the 20th century, when British visionaries like Gerald Gardner and Doreen Valiente began to publicize their involvement in Wiccan covens. Incidentally, some people believe Gardnerian Witchcraft was not so much the surviving remnant of an ancient lineage of Witches, but rather largely the invention of people like Valiente and Gardner. To me, this is an irrelevant quibble. Even if Gardner and his associates fabricated their tale of Witchcraft's ancient lineage, they still based their spirituality on the esoteric teachings of occult groups like the Golden Dawn; on folklore and mythology that speaks of ancient Pagan Gods and Goddesses; and on the wise woman tradition of village herbalists and healers, who from ancient to modern times have used shamanic practices to cure diseases and ensure a plentiful harvest. All of these magickal and spiritual elements have influenced the course of modern Wicca; so whether it is a genuine ancient lineage or merely a modern reconstruction of primitive practices, it has met the needs of hundreds of thousands of people, emerging as one of the fastest growing spiritual paths in recent years.

7 dimensions of the Craft

To help explain a bit more about Wiccan ways, I'd like to draw an analogy from the chakras. Chakra is a Sanskrit word that means "wheel of light," and it refers to numerous energy centers located within the human body/soul system. The seven main chakras are located along the spine, with the first located at the base of the spine, the second at the genital level, the third at the solar plexus, the fourth at the heart, the fifth at the vocal cords, the sixth at the forehead, and the seventh at the very top of the head (actually located above the head, at the crown of the soul). Each chakra controls a different energy pattern within the body and soul. Wicca can be understood in relation to the chakras. Indeed, one of the reasons why I find Wicca to be such a powerful spiritual path is because it equally honors and nurtures the energies of all seven chakras.

The first, or root chakra, governs our most basic connection to the earthly plane, to having a physical body with material needs. Like the first chakra, Wicca honors the basic goodness of Nature, the earth, and the physical world. Wicca does not see a separation or division between matter and spirit, but rather celebrates both as essentially one within the embrace of Goddess and God.

The second, or sacral chakra, governs our relationships and our sexuality. Like the second chakra, Wicca is a body-positive spiritual path. Wicca does not regard sex as dirty or sinful, but rather celebrates it as a gift of the Divine. In Wicca, taking good care of the body and enjoying responsible sexuality with a consenting adult partner is nothing to be ashamed of, but rather something to be celebrated. After all, since the Goddess and God are lovers, it is a good and sacred thing to enjoy passionate, loving sex with an appropriate partner.

The third, or solar plexus chakra, governs our connection to power. Like this chakra, Wicca encourages its practitioners to be mature, responsible, powerful people in their lives, their work, and their relationships. Wicca is a magickal religion—and magick can be defined as spiritual power. This is not the kind of power that controls or abuses people, but rather the power that comes from within to help each person to live life to its fullest potential. Many people think magick is about controlling other people (as in making someone fall in love with you against his or her will). But true magick is actually about everyone finding their own authentic, inner power. Thus, if I cast a love spell, I wouldn't be forcing someone else to love me against their will, but rather I'd be getting in touch with my own inner sexuality and attractiveness, which would make me become more naturally appealing to the right person.

The fourth, or heart chakra, governs our connection to love, compassion, and caring. Like this chakra, Wicca is a spirituality of love. "Perfect love and perfect trust" is the password to gain admission into traditional Wiccan circles—and it refers to the goal of every Wiccan student and initiate. Wicca celebrates love in all its forms: beginning with the Goddess and the God's love for us, our love for ourselves, our love for others, and love for Nature and the earth. As a loving spiritual path, it calls us to make wise and healthy choices in our lives. For example, how can someone litter or use energy wastefully, when she or he walks the path of loving the earth? So for Wiccans, love is not only a nice feeling, but a way of life.

The fifth, or throat chakra, governs our connection with communication and the arts. This chakra points to the creativity that Wicca encourages in people. The Craft is a spiritual path filled with songs and poetry, with artistic talent used to create dance, ritual, and objects of beauty. Most Witches enjoy expressing their spirituality in creative ways. Of course, there are as many ways to be creative as there are people. In addition to the artsy outlets like writing, music, or painting, other creative outlets include gardening, cooking, sewing, metalsmithing, brewing, and even parenting. Witches believe being creative is a way to express love to the Goddess and the God.

The sixth, or third eye chakra, governs mental ability, reasoning, and intelligence. Like this chakra, Wicca is a spiritual path that is friendly with science, philosophy, and human reason. Galileo would never have been imprisoned had he made his discoveries in a Wiccan culture, for Wicca advocates intellectual freedom and scientific inquiry. A person does not need to check his or her brain at the door when pursuing the Wiccan path. Of course, most Wiccans agree with Albert Einstein's statement, "Imagination is more important than knowledge." The scientific world of facts and figures needs to be balanced by the inner universe of imagination, poetry, and dreams. The point of the sixth chakra is that both realms are important. Scientific fact and poetic insight go hand in hand in the world of Wicca.

The seventh, or crown chakra, governs our connection with the Divine, eternity, Spirit guides, and the astral realm. This is the chakra of mysticism and soul wisdom. Like this chakra, Wicca is a mystical spirituality. Most Wiccans believe in the reality of the spirit world, and understand Spirit as encompassing the feminine Goddess and her consort, the masculine God. As important as the earth, the body, magick, love, creativity, and knowledge are to Wiccans, ultimately it is a spiritual path, about finding the deepest soul connection to the infinite source of all things.

There's much, much more to say about Wicca. This short chapter is meant only to provide a basic outline. To learn more, read on—and explore some of the books listed in the pages to come.

~ Part One ~
Discovering Wicca

The first step toward becoming a well-read Witch would naturally involve developing a thorough knowledge of Witchcraft. Although I believe the best approach to learning the old ways involves studying with a qualified Wiccan elder and participating in Craft rituals, reading about the old religion will deepen your experience of becoming a Witch. The books in the following five chapters provide beginning insights into Wicca and Paganism, along with intermediate and advanced Wiccan material, as well as a selection of Wiccan classics first published more than a generation ago. From learning how to cast a circle and understanding the wheel of the year, to in-depth surveys of Wiccan history or coven protocols—these are the books that cover the basics.

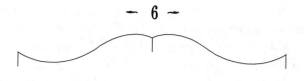

6

INTRODUCTORY BOOKS ON WICCA

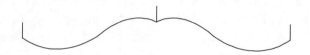

If you've never read a single book on Witchcraft and you couldn't tell the difference between an athame and an amulet, then these are the books for you. Again and again, these books explain why red represents Fire, but blue represents Water; they explain the difference between Samhain and Beltane; they patiently reassure readers that Witches have nothing to do with devil worship or Satanism, and so forth and so on.

Indeed, you might find that after you've read two or three of these introductory books, the rest start to seem pretty repetitive. At that point, it's tempting to move on to more advanced works. After all, once you're no longer a neophyte, dozens of other topics beckon—from herbalism to healing, from mythology to magick. Introductory books simply do not cover such beyond-the-beginner subjects in depth.

But even after you've read enough of these books that you can tell the difference between Lammas and Litha, I'd still recommend you explore most, if not all, of the books listed here. Why? Because different writers from different Craft traditions have diverse backgrounds, which mean their books inevitably depict Wicca in a colorful variety of ways. For example, Starhawk writes with the perceptive savvy of a political activist, while Janet and Stewart Farrar present their understanding of the old ways with down-home British charm. Vivianne Crowley, meanwhile, explores the Craft from the perspective of a Jungian psychologist. Each author writes from a distinctive lineage: Gardnerian, Alexandrian, Feminist, Celtic, Shamanic, Eclectic, Traditionalist, and other "flavors" of Wicca illuminate their words. If you'd like to have a truly comprehensive and universal view of the Craft, read as many of these books as possible.

Even after more than a decade of studying Wicca, I personally still love these books and others like them. When I recently discovered Fiona Horne's book (one of the newest listed here), it took me back to those mystical days years ago when I first read *The Spiral Dance*. Coming home to Wicca feels a lot like falling in love for the first time—it can evoke a sense of innocent happiness and joy. No matter how much of an elder Witch you may become in the future, the mysterious wonder of your first steps exploring this path will be something you'll always cherish. Reading a book for beginners, even when you're no longer one, can be a way to stay in touch with that wonder.

Starhawk
The Spiral Dance, A Rebirth of the Ancient Religion of the Great Goddess: Rituals, Invocations, Exercises, Magic, Twentieth Anniversary Edition

"Witchcraft has always been a religion of poetry, not theology," states Starhawk, who weaves throughout *The Spiral Dance* a poetic text combining intelligent scholarship with beautifully written, enjoyable prose. The author shows how Witchcraft is, first and foremost, a way to love the Goddess. Her strong feminist and political sensibilities play a large part in her descriptions of the Craft. She tends to regard the Goddess as the primary form of the Divine, but *The Spiral Dance* is by no means a women-only book. On the contrary, Starhawk emphasizes that Wicca is for everyone, male and female, straight and gay, white and non-white. While the political aspects of *The Spiral Dance* are provocative, this is more than just a textbook for activists. It's full of useful exercises, rituals, and visualizations, making it a valuable spiritual resource that continues to be useful for seasoned as well as neophyte Wiccans.

Janet and Stewart Farrar
A Witches' Bible: The Complete Witches' Handbook

If Starhawk provides the California ecofeminist perspective on Witchcraft, then the Farrars present a more traditionalist look at Wicca as it has developed in its homeland, the British Isles. *A Witches' Bible* is actually two books in one: *The Witches' Way* provides in-depth training in the philosophy of Wicca, while *Eight Sabbats For Witches* gives a detailed introduction to the history, lore, and ceremonial practices associated with each of the major Wiccan holidays. The Farrars' writing style is warm and accessible, while their knowledge of the old ways is thorough and perceptive.

Scott Cunningham
The Truth About Witchcraft Today

Here's the book to give to your mother when she wants to know why you've begun attending full moon rituals. Gently written and helpful even for those who have no desire to become Witches themselves, this introduction to Wicca covers the basics, from magick to mythology to ritual, with an emphasis on the ethics of the Wiccan Rede and the dispelling of misconceptions.

Vivianne Crowley
Wicca: The Old Religion in the New Millennium

"Wicca operates in two realms of truth—metaphysical truth and psychological truth," states Crowley in this intelligent and well-written introduction to the Craft. Where Starhawk explored the social and political dimensions of Wicca, Crowley (who is a Jungian psychologist) approaches the Craft more from a psychological perspective. In explaining the basics of the old religion, she explores the unity between metaphysical and psychological truth, considering the psychospiritual dynamics of magick and (especially) initiation.

Marion Weinstein
Positive Magic: Occult Self-Help

Magick is an essential part of Wicca, and often people who come to the Craft do so out of a desire to learn the ways of magick. This down-to-earth guide to magick as a doorway to Witchcraft (rather than the other way around), presents the basics in terms of magickal theory, the use of tools like astrology, Tarot, and affirmations (which Weinstein calls "Words of Power," a much more Witch-like term), along with a clear message about the importance of positive ethical standards.

Zsuzsanna Budapest
The Holy Book of Women's Mysteries: Feminist Witchcraft, Goddess Rituals, Spellcasting, & Other Womanly Arts

This is one of the most ardently feminist of Wiccan books. Although it was published in its present form in 1980, its roots go back a decade prior. It is now generally considered a Wiccan classic as well as the best introduction to the Dianic path. Among other pleasures, it includes an amusing essay by Starhawk on the "dangers" of magick.

Francesca De Grandis
Be A Goddess! A Guide to Celtic Spells and Wisdom for Self-Healing, Prosperity, and Great Sex

Healing, humor, and the love of the Goddess coalesce in this shimmering invitation to magickal ways. De Grandis, an initiate of the Faery Tradition and creator of the Third Road Tradition, has described herself as a "bardic brat" and a "vagabond shaman," reveling in one of the Craft's most joyful features—a sense of humor. *Be a Goddess!* provides 15 weekly lessons, with stories, rituals, prayers, and musings that give the reader a grounded introduction to Goddess Craft.

Fiona Horne,
Witch, A Magickal Journey: A Hip Guide to Modern Witchcraft

Punk rocker/radio personality Fiona Horne is a young, funky, body-positive solitary Witch; she's into snakes and tattoos and presents the Craft in a playful but outspoken way. Horne's writing style does tend to be a bit on the cutesy side—for example, she likes to use the adjective "witchy." An excellent primer for those who don't feel a natural kinship to the granola-esque culture that has grown around Witchcraft ever since it became an unofficial hippie religion back in the 1960s and 70s.

Patricia Crowther
Lid Off the Cauldron: A Wicca Handbook

Written in a folksy, down-to-earth style by a priestess initiated in the early 1960s by Gerald Gardner himself, this book presents Wicca as a living British tradition. The last few chapters provide rituals corresponding to each of the planets, showing how Wicca can provide a ritual complement to occult practices such as astrology.

Raymond Buckland
Buckland's Complete Book of Witchcraft

A true workbook, this guide includes 15 lessons, each of which ends with questions designed to reinforce the material and assist the student in mastering the basics of the Craft. There's even a set of examination questions in the back of the book (with a separate section for answers). This blends traditional British Craft with a more contemporary, self-initiatory approach, making it useful for both solitaries and groups.

Lady Sabrina
Exploring Wicca: The Beliefs, Rites, and Rituals of the Wiccan Religion

A concise book full of useful information, *Exploring Wicca* gives an overview of the symbolism and lore of Wicca, along with basic instruction in spellcraft, a list of resources, and a recommended reading list. The author considers both the devotional (religious) and functional (magickal) dimensions of the Craft.

Marian Green
A Witch Alone: Thirteen Moons to Master Natural Magic

Joining a coven may not always be the best choice for those who wish to practice the old ways. Solitary Witches stand in a long tradition of shamans, village healers, and wise women whose knowledge of herbal cures made them an invaluable part of society. Traditionally solitaries learned as apprentices from elder solitaries. This book can help today's loner Witch master the basic skills of the old ways, even when no teacher may be readily available.

Phyllis Curott
Book of Shadows: A Modern Woman's Journey into the Wisdom of Witchcraft and the Magic of the Goddess

An answer to skeptics who think Witchcraft amounts to nothing more than a bunch of angry teenagers who like to dress in black. Curott, a successful Manhattan lawyer, defies the stereotype of Wiccans as mere adolescent rebels. This memoir, filled with mythic undertones, makes a compelling argument for the Craft as an intelligent, viable spirituality for modern times.

– 7 –

Introductory Books on Paganism

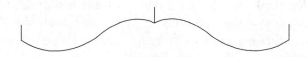

Not long ago, I was explaining to a group of young Wiccans why I embraced Nature spirituality. I said that for me, supporting an independent Pagan community is like shopping at a locally owned family business, whereas membership in a Christian church seems more like patronizing an anonymous mega-conglomerate chain-store run by people from other parts of the country (or world) who could care less about the unique needs of our local community. My friends were stunned at the analogy—and yet all I was doing was retelling a point made over 20 years ago by Margot Adler in her book on Paganism, *Drawing Down the Moon*. This incident made me realize just how valuable books are—as custodians of the wisdom of our elders—and how necessary it is for each new generation to read the books and claim that wisdom as their own.

To understand Wicca, we need to explore the larger spiritual renaissance known as Paganism (or Neopaganism). Wicca is a form of Paganism—Wicca is to Paganism what Zen is to Buddhism or Lutheranism is to Christianity. Just as not all Buddhists practice Zen, so not all who call themselves Pagans identify as Witches or Wiccans (for that matter, not all Wiccans like being called Pagan, mainly because they want to be clear that their spiritual path differs from that of Druids or other Nature mystics). Paganism has been reborn in our industrial/technological culture because of a burning desire felt by so many people who wish to reconnect with Nature and the spirituality of our ancestors. Wicca is one marvelous answer to that desire, but as the books profiled in this chapter show, it is certainly not the only option.

If the books in Chapter 6 demonstrated how much diversity exists among the traditions of Wicca, the titles in this chapter reveal that even more differences can be found among the many varieties of Paganism. Paganism encompasses not only Witchcraft and Goddess spirituality, but also shamanism, Druidism, other forms of primal religion, and even countercultural forms of spirituality like the psychedelic mysticism of Terence McKenna and the back-to-Nature community called the Rainbow Family. The counterculturalists may not even like being labeled Pagan, since they regard spirituality as something beyond all the limitations of religion, institutionalism, and societal labels. But that, ironically, is one of the ways in which they fit in to the Pagan mold, for most Pagans tend to be intelligent, fiercely individualistic, and disinclined to accept other peoples' definitions of who they are.

Margot Adler
Drawing Down the Moon: Witches, Druids, Goddess-Worshippers, and Other Pagans in America Today, Revised and expanded edition

This brilliant book combines keen psychological insight with a journalist's ability to report on complex material in a clear, easy-to-understand way. Adler's deft unraveling of the Pagan knot explores not only the spiritual principles that undergird the movement, but considers its larger social, political, and cultural implications as well. As the largest "flavor" of Paganism, Wicca understandably gets the most attention in this book. But Adler succeeds in illustrating the diversity within the Nature spirituality community; as she considers Druids, Egyptian, and Greek revivalists; non-Wiccan Goddess communities; the Church of All Worlds (based on the vision of Robert Heinlein's science fiction masterpiece *Stranger in a Strange Land*); and even satirical groups like the Erisians and the Discordians.

Drawing Down the Moon was published in 1979 and revised in 1986. It is primarily a work of journalism, a snapshot of Paganism taken in the late 70s and retouched a bit in the mid-80s. Today, it unfortunately feels dated. The author reports how much had changed in the Pagan world between 1979 and 1986, leaving the reader to wonder how much more has occurred in the ensuing years. Still, for its sheer readability, incisive analysis, and comprehensive reporting, this remains an essential book.

Vivianne Crowley
Phoenix from the Flame: Pagan Spirituality in the Western World

Sort of a British *Drawing Down the Moon* for the new generation, this overview of Paganism concentrates especially on Druidic, Nordic, and Wiccan expressions of Nature spirituality, with generous sections on each of those communities. After considering the history, philosophy, and experience of today's Pagans, Crowley speculates on what directions the Pagan path may take in the future.

Graham Harvey and Charlotte Hardman
Paganism Today: Wiccans, Druids, the Goddess and Ancient Earth Traditions for the Twenty-First Century

A collection of writings from a number of different authors, divided into two sections: "Main Traditions in Contemporary Paganism," which explores the various flavors of Paganism, and "Paganism in Practice," which considers issues such as group dynamics, the role of tradition, the practice of ritual, and the politics of gender within the Pagan world.

Prudence Jones and Caitlín Matthews, editors
Voices From the Circle: The Heritage of Western Paganism

Several leading figures in the Pagan community, including Philip Carr-Gomm, R. J. Stewart, and Vivianne Crowley, contributed to this collection of essays exploring various facets of modern Nature spirituality. Shamanism, Druidry, Goddess worship, Wicca, and traditional Witchcraft are all represented here in articles exploring the dynamics of initiation, the wisdom of animals, and the magickal symbolism of the circle.

Ellen Evert Hopman and Lawrence Bond
People of the Earth: The New Pagans Speak Out: Interviews with Margot Adler, Starhawk, Susun Weed, Z. Budapest, and Many Others

An anthology of interviews with a wide variety of Pagans, from the celebrities mentioned in the subtitle to more ordinary folks, who represent different traditions, lifestyles, and experiences. Talks with mainstream Pagans (Druids, Witches, and so forth) stand next to conversations with more unusual personalities, such as military Pagans, political activists, and sacred prostitutes.

Loretta Orion
Never Again the Burning Times: Paganism Revived

An ethnographic study of American Neopaganism, tracing its growth from its roots in British Wicca. Orion explores issues related to magick and healing, two areas of keen interest to Wiccans and Pagans in general. Some of the most fascinating research in this book considers the relationship Pagans have with mainstream healthcare.

Philip Carr-Gomm, editor
The Druid Renaissance: the Voice of Druidry Today

A comprehensive introduction to the modern Pagan Druid movement, which combines Nature spirituality with the lore of ancient Celtic wisdom. Modern Druids attune themselves deeply to the natural world, devoted to the Gods and Goddesses of the Celtic people, and dedicated to honoring their ancestors (both spiritually and physically). Like Wiccans, Druids see themselves as embodying an authentically European form of shamanism. This book includes information about Druids in the British Isles, North America, and France, with emphasis on Druidry's philosophical and ecological dimensions.

Maya Magee Sutton, Ph.D., and Nicholas R. Mann
Druid Magic: The Practice of Celtic Wisdom

Emma Restall Orr
Spirits of the Sacred Grove: The World of a Druid Priestess

Two more books on modern Druidry. *Druid Magic* provides a practical, hands-on approach to practicing the Druid path today, while *Spirits of the Sacred Grove* recounts the experience of Druid spirituality from the perspective of a Grove priestess.

Mara Freeman
Kindling the Celtic Spirit: Ancient Traditions to Illumine Your Life Throughout the Seasons

A beautifully-designed book that deftly avoids labels like Pagan or Druid, this celebration of modern ways to observe Celtic tradition nevertheless falls squarely within the Pagan sphere. The chapters (one for each month of the year) include mythic stories, recipes, tales of Goddesses, trees, and beasts, and simple ritual practices easily incorporated into the home.

Freya Aswynn
Northern Mysteries and Magick: Runes, Gods, and Feminine Powers

Rune master Freya Aswynn provides an overview of Norse shamanism and Paganism in this introductory text. While most of the material presented here involves use of the runes, the book also contains a directory of Norse Gods and Goddesses as well as a glimpse into Norse feminine mysteries (especially helpful for those who may think of Norse Paganism as patriarchal; it's an unfair stereotype that comes from modern interpreters of Nordic ways). This is a revision of Aswynn's *Leaves of Yggdrasil*; this new version beats the original because it includes a CD of shamanic chanting based on the northern mysteries.

Michael I. Niman
People of the Rainbow: A Nomadic Utopia

A glimpse into the culture of the Rainbow Family, a community that since the early 1970s has created an alternative way of life through regional and national gatherings at national forests and other remote settings. Loosely organized around principles of nonviolence, environmentalism, consensus government, and a barter economy, Rainbows endorse no religious dogma, but can be considered Pagan in their openness to Nature mysticism, magick, and spiritual freedom.

Terence McKenna
The Archaic Revival: Speculations on Psychedelic Mushrooms, the Amazon, Virtual Reality, UFOs, Evolution, Shamanism, the Rebirth of the Goddess, and the End of History

A true visionary whose mind was soaked in psilocybin, McKenna saw the resurgence of primal practices, from Goddess spirituality to the throbbing rhythms of rock 'n' roll, as the raw material of humanity's quest for salvation from the deadly excesses of modern technology. This book helps connect the dots between the hippie counterculture and the worldwide resurgence of Pagan ways.

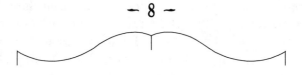

8

INTERMEDIATE WICCAN BOOKS

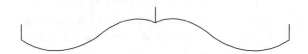

Once upon a time, few books on Wicca existed beyond the introductory titles by celebrity Witches such as Sybil Leek and Gerald Gardner. I know a Wiccan elder who jokes, "When I was first getting interested in the Craft, there were only six books available on the subject!" He's exaggerating (a bit), but it's true that once upon a time the number of titles available were relatively few, while today a veritable publishing explosion is underway, with dozens of new Wiccan books coming out every year. While most of these books are still aimed at the novice or newcomer, increasing numbers of titles are appearing that assume the reader has at least some background in the old ways.

The books included in this section are examples of how Wiccan writing has expanded beyond the beginner level. While some of these books do contain introductory material, these are titles that include information useful for the advanced student or even the first-degree initiate. These books take the reader beyond the basics of casting a circle or explaining the Sabbats. As is often the case with beyond-the-beginner material, some of the subjects touched upon in these books are controversial within the Craft community; authors like Ellen Cannon Reed or Frederic Lamond present ideas within their books that are not always warmly received by all segments of the Pagan community. So be it. To be a well-read Witch involves exposure to more than one particular viewpoint. Some of the books reviewed here (and in subsequent chapters) will present ideas sharply in conflict with one another. My goal is to introduce you to books with important things to say. As the reader, you get to decide which books, if any, present viewpoints you can support.

If you're a beginner, I recommend you start with the introductory books. After all, there's plenty of wonderful material to be found in the books profiled in the last two chapters. But once you have a strong sense of the basics, these are excellent books to help you as you seek to deepen your spiritual practice.

Francesca De Grandis
Goddess Initiation: A Practical Celtic Program for Soul-Healing, Self-Fulfillment and Wild Wisdom

Traditional Witches study for at least a year and a day before undergoing initiation into the Craft; but today many people have no access to an elder who can train them. Francesca De Grandis's *Goddess Initiation* provides a thorough, powerful, and structured program of self-preparation for entry into the mysteries. As in her first book, De Grandis combines a playful writing style with a keen insight into the processes necessary for true spiritual growth. Her program is safe for the inexperienced seeker, yet has enough substance to be challenging and insightful even for those whose spiritual journey is well underway. Even if you're working with a teacher and will receive your initiation through your teacher's lineage, De Grandis's wise words can help you along the way.

Ellen Cannon Reed
The Heart of Wicca: Wise Words from a Crone on the Path

A collection of brief meditations on what Wicca is, what it could be, and what it is in danger of becoming—thanks to the impact of so many books, TV shows, and Web sites that seem to present Wicca as a spiritual fashion statement rather than as a powerful system for magickal transformation. Reed envisions Wicca as a dynamic and elegant program of initiation into the mysteries—it's not about politics, it's not about fashion, it's not about do-your-own-thing spirituality. As such, her ideas often fly in the face of contemporary Pagan culture. But her views are thought-provoking and important not only for the Wiccan traditionalist who will agree with her devotion to the mysteries and the initiatory path, but for everyone who wants a full experience of the depth of Wiccan spirituality.

Ellen Cannon Reed
The Witches Tarot

Ellen Cannon Reed
The Witches Qabala: The Pagan Path and the Tree of Life

After learning the basics of Wicca, a logical path for serious students is to begin studying the Western Mystery Tradition—the grand history of occult philosophy that dates back to philosophers of antiquity. Two of the most important branches of the Western Tradition are the Qabala (a body of esoteric teachings that originated in Jewish mysticism, but became embraced by magickal groups like the Golden Dawn) and the Tarot (far more than a mere deck of fortune telling cards, the Tarot includes powerful symbols that correspond with the magickal philosophy of the Qabala). Written especially for Wiccans, Reed's books are perfect for anyone who is a beginner at studying these magickal systems.

Robin Wood
When, Why . . . If: An Ethics Workbook

Robin Wood is an artist, and her eponymous Tarot deck has been warmly embraced by the Pagan community as a wonderful re-visioning of the Tarot using almost exclusively Nature- and Goddess-based imagery. But this book might be Wood's most enduring contribution to the Craft. Because Wicca only has one ethical principle ("if it harms none, do what you will"), for some it may be too easy to overlook the vital role that values such as honesty, helpfulness, sexual responsibility, and compassionate love play in the Craft. This charming and down-to-earth book goes a long way toward reinforcing a truly Pagan system of ethics.

Charles G. Leland
Aradia, or the Gospel of the Witches

This late 19th century manuscript reveals the practices and teachings of Italian Witches, as documented by Leland, an American folklorist. This book includes the earliest documented appearance of the Charge of the Goddess, with charms and spells and prayers for the Lady, especially in the forms of Diana and her daughter, Aradia, who came to the earth to be the teacher of the Witches.

Raven Grimassi
The Wiccan Mysteries: Ancient Origins & Teachings
Raven Grimassi
Wiccan Magick: Inner Teachings of the Craft

These books explore the distinction between learning the secrets and experiencing the mysteries. Grimassi plumbs the mystical and magickal depths of Witchcraft, emphasizing how it functions as a mystery religion (a system in which seekers are initiated into profound experiences of divine truth, truth that cannot be intellectually transmitted through books or words but can only be experienced through ritual or meditation). These books hint at how much more there is to Wicca than appears on the surface.

Janus-Mithras, Nuit-Hilaria, and Mer-Amun
Wicca: The Ancient Way

This slender little book (64 pages) is out of print and probably rather hard to find, as it never had major distribution. But it is well worth seeking out (see Chapter 38 for tips on locating used books). "The purpose of this book is to acquaint the reader with the existence of a living, initiated and traditional mystery religion." The tradition being discussed is the Isis Urania tradition, which traces its lineage back before the initiation of Gerald Gardner. If you've never heard of this particular lineage, don't be surprised; often traditionalist Witches like to maintain a low profile, thinking it best not to publish material related to their tradition—making this book a rarity. Of course, true to its lineage, the book reveals nothing in the way of initiatory secrets. With chapters on the three degree system, the God and Goddess, the Mighty Ones, and the grand Sabbat of All-Hallows Eve, it provides a basic, sometimes opinionated, but entirely authentic glimpse into one of the most traditional forms of the Craft.

Gwyn
Light from the Shadows, A Mythos of Modern Traditional Witchcraft

Another glimpse of Witchcraft in its most traditional form, especially as practiced in the British Isles. Although organized around basic topics ranging from the tools of the Craft to the Wheel of the Year, it's helpful for the reader who wants to go a little bit deeper than the bare essentials as found in a beginner's book.

Patricia Telesco
A Charmed Life: Celebrating Wicca Every Day

A down-to-earth book by a self-proclaimed "militant Kitchen Witch" who encourages the reader to find ways to practice the Craft as a regular day-to-day part of life—from cultivating environmental awareness, to magickal dimensions of personal finance, to incorporating Wiccan observances into a family's ordinary routine.

Frederic Lamond
Religion Without Beliefs: Essays in Pantheist Theology, Comparative Religion and Ethics

Lamond was initiated into Gerald Gardner's coven in 1957 and remains active in the London Pagan community over 40 years later. His book is less of a how-to about Wicca and more of a vigorous philosophical argument for Nature-based spirituality. He looks at social, political, and theological forces in our society, and argues for the value of a religion based not in revealed teachings (like a sacred book) but rather in the wisdom inherent in the natural world.

Lady Sara
The Book of Light

Another out of print title that's well worth tracking down. One elder told me, "Back in the 70s when everyone was reading Lady Sheba, those who were in the know read Lady Sara instead." *The Book of Light* is essentially a grimoire with information on herbs, oils, scents, various ritual spells, along with astrological information and tables of correspondences.

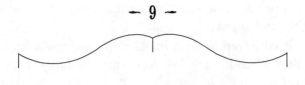

9

ADVANCED
WICCAN BOOKS

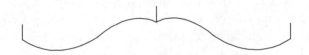

If beginner books are for novices and intermediate books are for those who have made a commitment to the Wiccan path, advanced books are of particular use to Witches whose commitment and seniority places them in positions of leadership, as elders, teachers, and high priests and priestesses.

The books in this chapter do not convey much in the way of Wiccan secrets; few, if any, elders would ever feel comfortable imparting the deepest secrets of their tradition to the general public. Indeed, I personally tend to be skeptical of any author who claims to reveal all the hidden secrets of ancient Witchcraft—chances are, the author is either not telling the truth, or simply does not know the full extent of Wiccan mysticism. At its core, Wicca is not about secrets so much as about mysteries, and the mysteries of the Goddess cannot be captured in a book. They can only be experienced through life.

The best a book can do is point out to us that such experiential mysteries do exist—but they exist in a place beyond words, thought, and language.

So if advanced Wiccan books don't give away all the secrets, then what do they do? Well, they primarily support the Wiccan elder in his or her work. The first three books in this section provide practical guidance on topics like running a coven or learning how to invoke the Goddess and the God. Take coven leadership, for example. It's amazing how much work is involved in keeping even a small group of three to 13 people together, functioning smoothly, while enabling each person to grow spiritually. To have a healthy and successful group takes a lot of effort, from keeping things organized to being an intuitive spiritual mentor. And while lineaged Witches will have the guidance of their elders in administering a coven, even they can benefit from the sensible advice of writers like Amber K and Judy Harrow.

Other books on this list explore the history of the Craft, ranging from a controversial consideration of an alleged Witch from the 19th century to two in-depth looks at the life and work of Gerald Gardner. Finally, a few of the titles listed here are scholarly in nature. Such works are useful, as they shed light on what academics think of Nature religion. Sure, the dry scholarly prose sometimes makes for a boring read, but these books do provide insight into the Craft as a spiritual megatrend of our times.

Amber K
Covencraft: Witchcraft for Three or More

Five hundred pages of reference material for those who would lead (or start) a coven. Amber K does not particularly endorse starting your own group, but recognizes that many people will do just that, often for perfectly valid reasons (there's no existing coven within driving distance). For those who are, in effect, reinventing the wheel, this book can help to dodge some of the pitfalls along the way. And even for those who start their own group after training in an existing coven, this volume is full of useful information on topics such as administration, conflict management, finding new members, training, and preventing burnout among coven elders.

Judy Harrow
Wicca Covens: How to Start and Organize Your Own

More insights into the task of leading a Wiccan group. Includes practical information (what to do about childcare) along with considerations of the different roles that a coven can play in people's lives: coven as a chosen family, as a magickal growth and a support group, as a place for training and education, and so forth. There's also a chapter on working partnerships, for those who are co-leading a group (often, but not always, as Priestess and Priest).

Lady Maeve Rhea
Summoning Forth Wiccan Gods and Goddesses: The Magick of Invocation and Evocation

A disarmingly simple introduction to the magick of invocation (calling the Goddess or other spiritual being into one's self) and evocation (calling a spiritual being into something other than the self, such as into a specially marked space). The summoning of spiritual beings is central to the mystery of Wicca, and this book, while short and quite basic, treats its subject with reverence and thoughtful care. The exercises are carefully written to guide the beginner to a safe, structured experience of contact with the Deities and other beings. Although written for the solitary, I think this would be useful for initiates studying in a coven setting who want support in developing their magickal and ritual skills.

Ronald Hutton
The Triumph of the Moon: A History of Modern Pagan Witchcraft

A brilliantly written, thoroughly researched, and carefully balanced history of Wicca, that succeeds both as an academic treatise as well as a useful reference for Craft practitioners. Hutton considers numerous sources of the modern Craft, including Freemasonry, Occultism, the village wise woman tradition, and changing attitudes toward Goddess spirituality and Paganism in 19th and 20th century Britain. He then focuses particularly on Gerald Gardner before documenting the many public Wiccan figures who emerged after Gardner. I consider this book to be required reading for anyone who wants an intellectually honest and thorough overview of modern Wiccan history.

Philip Heselton
Wiccan Roots: Gerald Gardner and the Modern Witchcraft Revival

A detailed consideration of the circumstances surrounding the initiation of Gerald Gardner into Wicca, probably in the fall of 1939, as well as a look at the Lammas 1940 rites performed by British Witches to protect Britain from a Nazi invasion. The author considers who the key players were in this critical chapter of Witch history. Read this after or along with Ronald Hutton's *The Triumph of the Moon*.

W. E. Liddell and Michael Howard
The Pickingill Papers: The Origin of the Gardnerian Craft

A controversial collection of essays published in two British Pagan magazines that claim to document the existence of Witch covens in eastern England dating back to the 18th century, centered around a village healer named George Pickingill

(1816-1909). In *The Triumph of the Moon*, Ronald Hutton considers at length how believable these papers are, but stops short at issuing a verdict.

Aidan A. Kelly
Crafting the Art of Magic, Book 1: A History of Modern Witchcraft, 1939-1964

Ten years after this book was published, it is out of print, and Book 2 has never materialized. But even without a sequel, this book is valuable simply because it contains all the various versions of Gardner's Book of Shadows. Kelly does a lot of speculating on the details and circumstances of Gerald Gardner's life as the world's first public Wiccan, and not all of his speculations are complimentary to Gardner.

Bengt Ankarloo and Stuart Clark, editors
Witchcraft and Magic in Europe (six volume series)

This magisterial series gathers together scholarly essays on the history of Paganism, the Occult, and Witchcraft, covering the sweep of European history from Biblical and Paleopagan times to the 20th century. Reflecting their academic rather than spiritual orientation, these books define "Witchcraft" as encompassing more than just Wicca, but also includes devil worship and malevolent Sorcery. However, the final volume of the series is fair in its depiction of Wicca as a benevolent spirituality which became popular in the 20th century, and clearly distinguishes Wicca from Satanism. If nothing else, the material presented here provides a profound study of how Witchcraft as a cultural concept has developed and evolved over the years, and as such is invaluable to any historian of the Craft.

Helen A. Berger
A Community of Witches: Contemporary Neo-Paganism and Witchcraft in the United States

James R. Lewis, editor
Magical Religion and Modern Witchcraft

Joanne Pearson, Richard H. Roberts, and Geoffrey Samuels, editors
Nature Religion Today: Paganism in the Modern World

Three examples of the increasing attention sociologists, anthropologists, and scholars of religion are paying to the Wiccan community. Sometimes, the learned tone of these books is annoying (such as when Berger has to speculate on whether Paganism really fits the scholarly definition of a religion or not), and for the reader who wants more understanding of Craft mysteries, don't waste your time here. But if you're interested in what the Ivory Tower has to say about Nature spirituality, these books will fill you in.

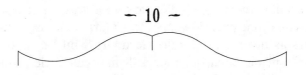

10

WICCAN CLASSICS
(PUBLISHED BEFORE 1979)

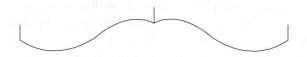

The year 1979 was a watershed time for Wicca, at least in North America. Samhain (October 31) of that year marked the publication of two books reviewed in previous chapters: Starhawk's *The Spiral Dance* (Chapter 6) and Margot Adler's *Drawing Down the Moon* (Chapter 7). These books brought Nature spirituality to a new and larger audience, mainly by lifting Wicca out of its identity as an occult practice and showing how it fits within the larger societal trends of feminism, environmentalism, and the New Age movement. Starhawk's work explains how feminists could revere the Goddess as a symbol of women's power, and even non-sexist men could celebrate the horned God as a positive, anti-patriarchal male role model. Adler's book demonstrates how Wicca is but one aspect of the larger Pagan revival, and draws clear connections linking Pagan spirituality with both environmentalism and New Age mysticism.

So in many ways, 1979 marked a turning point for Wicca. It was still early in the Craft's modern history: Starhawk's first book came out only 20 years after Gardner's last. Although writers as diverse as Gerald Gardner, Sybil Leek, and Leo Martello made an impact, especially in occult circles, with their books about the old religion, the Wiccan community had not yet produced a manifesto with the potential widespread appeal of *The Spiral Dance*. Yet once that book appeared, it literally changed everything: one did not need to be an Occultist to find the Wiccan path. Today Wicca is thought of as an *alternative* spiritual path; we forget that before 1979, it was more truly an *underground* spirituality—occult, after all, means "hidden."

Underground and hidden, perhaps, but not entirely invisible. While relatively few Wiccan books were published in the quarter century before 1979, a significant number of those books have become established classics in the literature of the modern Craft. When I say a book is a classic, I don't necessarily mean a bestseller or even that it is currently available: indeed, several of the books listed in this chapter are, as of this writing, out of print (see Chapter 38 for a few hints on how to locate out of print books). These are the books that present-day Wiccan historians, like Ronald Hutton, have relied on to help describe the early years of the movement. Today's Wiccan leaders often recommend the titles profiled in this chapter because these were the books they themselves read back when they were students. These books most obviously demonstrate that Wicca is a religion of tradition, for these are the voices of our elders—and it is out of the words of the elders that tradition emerges. Incidentally, the dates given are dates of first publication, to give you a sense of how old these books are.

Gerald Gardner
A Goddess Arrives (1939)
Scire (Gerald Gardner)
High Magic's Aid (1949)

Gerald Gardner
Witchcraft Today (1954)

Gerald Gardner
The Meaning of Witchcraft (1959)

Books by the man who first brought Witchcraft into the public eye. *A Goddess Arrives* and *High Magic's Aid* are novels; hardly great literature, but remarkable for their presentation of Goddess devotion and Witchcraft respectively as subjects worthy of serious modern spiritual inquiry. Finally, in 1954, came *Witchcraft Today*, where the author is identified as "member of one of the ancient covens of the Witch cult, which still survives in England." Written in a rambly, folksy style, ranging from the anthropology of the Fairies to the occult mysteries surrounding the Knights' Templar, this is hardly a carefully organized book about Witchcraft, but rather a glimpse into a colorful mind. Perhaps the most useful of Gardner's books was his final work, *The Meaning of Witchcraft*, which provides an in-depth exploration of the roots of Wicca, including material on the Druids, Stone Age shamanism, and Witchcraft in Roman and Saxon times.

Patricia Crowther
Witch Blood! The Diary of a Witch High Priestess (1974)

Memoir from one of Gardner's better-known initiates, who wrote *Lid Off the Cauldron*. She also wrote a more recent autobiography called *One Witch's World* (Robert Hale, 1998).

Alex Sanders
The Alex Sanders Lectures (1970)

June Johns
King of the Witches: The World of Alex Sanders (1969)

After Gardner's death and Sybil Leek's departure for America, the founder of the Alexandrian tradition became the most well-known British Witch, the epicenter of the burgeon-ing Wiccan scene in 1960s London. Several authors wrote about Sanders and his wife Maxine, including Margot Adler (*Drawing Down the Moon*) and Stewart Farrar (*What Witches Do*). June Johns's *King of the Witches* was the first such book to feature Sanders and the only one devoted entirely to telling his story. Unlike so many of the Wiccan-priests-turned-authors, Sanders wrote no book; his own words are memorialized only in *The Alex Sanders Lectures*, a slim collection of a dozen talks from the early 70s.

Justine Glass
Witchcraft, the Sixth Sense, and Us (1965)

Early consideration of Wicca from a non-Wiccan author, including some controversial material on Robert Cochrane, a figure who advocated traditionalist (in contrast to Gardnerian or Alexandrian) Wicca in the 1960s. As the title implies, this book emphasizes the psychic dimension of Witchcraft. If for no other reason, get it for the frontispiece—a photograph of Doreen Valiente and Patricia Crowther in full Wiccan regalia.

Stewart Farrar
What Witches Do: The Modern Coven Revealed (1971)

In the 1980s, Stewart Farrar, along with his wife Janet, wrote the tremendously useful *A Witches' Bible* (profiled in Chapter 6). *A Witches' Bible* speaks with the authority of Craft elders, whereas *What Witches Do*, Stewart's first book on Wicca, sparkles with the excitement and enthusiasm of a newly initiated Witch. Originally commissioned as a journal-istic assignment, *What Witches Do* recounts how Farrar fell in love with the old religion and was ultimately initiated by Alex and Maxine Sanders. Along with telling of Farrar's spiri-tual journey, the book provides an entertaining and readable introduction to Wicca.

Sybil Leek
Diary of a Witch (1968)

Sybil Leek
The Complete Art of Witchcraft: Penetrating the Mystery Behind Magic Powers (1975)

In the 1960s, Sybil Leek enjoyed widespread celebrity as a Witch. She wrote books on a variety of metaphysical topics, but these two remain her most enduring Wiccan titles. Her auto-biographical *Diary of a Witch* has a charming, folksy feel to it. *The Complete Art* suffers because of a less-than-enlightened chapter on the role of homosexuality in Wicca—even though the Craft as a whole is deeply tolerant of sexual diversity, Leek saw same-sex love as a problem to be solved. Even so, many traditionalist Wiccans love this book because of its insistence that Wicca requires far more than merely joining (or forming) an occult study group.

Leo Louis Martello
Witchcraft: The Old Religion (1973)

A curious tour through the landscape of Wiccan culture, part appreciation for figures like Gardner, Murray, and Leland, and part rumination on subjects such as horns (as in the Horned God), with interviews of several Wiccan priests and priest-esses thrown into the soup. Martello founded the Witches Anti-Defamation League, an early attempt at creating a national advocacy group for Wiccans, and wrote books not only on Witchcraft, but also on divination and psychic phenomena.

Lady Sheba
The Grimoire of Lady Sheba (1972)

A basic collection of rituals, recipes, and laws. Llewellyn republished Lady Sheba's *Grimoire* in 2001; prior to that, cop-ies of this book were only available through rare booksellers on the Internet who often could fetch $100 or more for a copy. It's worth having, if only for its place in the history of Wiccan literature. A paperback version of Lady Sheba's *Book of Shadows* is also available, but the *Grimoire* contains the entire *Book of Shadows*, so that's the smarter book to buy.

Doreen Valiente
Witchcraft for Tomorrow (1973)

Doreen Valiente
An ABC of Witchcraft Past and Present (1978)

The first two books by Gardner's High Priestess, who is generally regarded as having been the author of many key Wiccan texts (such as the "Witches' Rune"), although often without credit. *An ABC* is a handy book that presents various tidbits of information in a dictionary format, while *Witchcraft For Tomorrow* includes Valiente's Book of Shadows.

Ray Buckland
Witchcraft From the Inside: Origins of the Fastest Growing Religious Movement in America (1971)

Ray Buckland
Ancient and Modern Witchcraft: the Truth About Witchcraft By A Witch High Priest (1970)

Two books by one of the first Gardnerian priests to come to America (and the author of *Buckland's Complete Book of Witchcraft*). Buckland has been a prolific author, producing works on candle magick, color magick, and Scottish Witchcraft. These two books are more general in their focus, considering the Craft as a whole.

~ Part Two ~
The Elements of
Wicca

After reading through the introductory books on Witch-craft, those who wish to become dedicants of the old ways may find it frustrating that so many Witch books simply rehash the most basic tenets of the Craft. Where can the intermediate student turn to continue her or his education? Perhaps by studying the various elements of Wicca in greater depth, the seeker can find new opportunities for growth and development. Exploring these elements—topics like psychic development, herbalism and healing, or the mythology of the Goddess and the God—may involve reading some books that are not Wiccan at all (at least on the surface). Not to worry. If a book's subject matter proves relevant to the Craft, then it is one that a well-read Witch will probably enjoy.

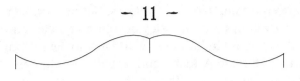

11

THE GODDESS

The single most important characteristic of Wicca is its devotion to the Goddess.

I find it amusing that Goddess spirituality has become so much of a fad in recent years. Go into any New Age or metaphysical bookstore, and you will see Goddess jewelry, Goddess t-shirts, all sorts of Goddess books (many of which on the surface appear to have nothing to do with Wicca), and even flavors of incense and oils named after various Goddesses. I sometimes think Wiccans ought to wear t-shirts that say "I worshiped the Goddess before Goddess worship was cool!" After all, Wicca is largely responsible for this groundswell of Goddess devotion. Demeter, Aphrodite, and Kuan Yin might still be sleeping, were it not for the work of Witches to awaken them.

Just who is the Goddess, and why does she have so many names? Two schools of thought exist among various Pagans and Wiccans, what I would describe as the polytheistic view and the unified view. Basically, polytheistic Pagans don't believe in a single over-arching God or Goddess, but acknowledge many deities to whom they can offer devotion and call on for aid. Thus, the various Goddesses of world mythology—from Isis, to Hathor, to Hera, to Artemis, and on and on—all represent different spiritual beings, different deities. Within this view, it's not polite to think that Kali and Freya and Rhea and so forth are really just "all the same Goddess." Deities are like people: every one is unique, and each one wants to be treated as an individual. Such polytheistic thinking is a minority view, but some Pagans hold it.

The unified view, more common among Wiccans, tends to view the various Goddesses (and Gods) of world mythology as many different faces of a single Ultimate Divine. "All Gods are one God, and all Goddesses are one Goddess" is a common expression of this view. This position accepts mythology as just that—myth, not necessarily of any historical truth but valuable in spiritual ways—and often sees the Goddess and the God themselves as but two sides of the same coin: two aspects of a single Divine Source who transcends human gender altogether, what mystics have called the Godhead.

Ultimately, whether you regard the Goddess as one ultimate manifestation of the Divine Feminine, or as a shorthand way of thinking about all the various polytheistic Goddesses of the world over, is a matter of personal preference and coven tradition. Because Wicca values experience before theology, what matters most is what all Pagans share in common, a commitment to understanding, experiencing, and revering the Sacred in feminine (as well as masculine) ways.

These books celebrate Goddess spirituality in a variety of ways, ranging from personal devotion to scholarly knowledge. Taken as a whole, they provide a wealth of resources to everyone who considers devotion to the Divine Feminine as central to their spiritual practice.

Elinor W. Gadon
The Once and Future Goddess: A Sweeping Visual Chronicle of the Sacred Female and Her Reemergence in the Cultural Mythology of Our Time

Not only does this work document 30,000 years of Goddess history as it traces the Divine Feminine from prehistoric cult figurines to postmodern spirituality, it also celebrates the Goddess as an inspiring figure within artistic culture. Illustrations of artistic depictions of the Goddess, ancient and contemporary, throughout this book drive home the essential link between matriarchal spirituality and creativity.

Carol P. Christ
Laughter of Aphrodite: Reflections on a Journey to the Goddess

The story of how one woman underwent a transition from the patriarchal religion of her youth and her education to embracing the renaissance of Goddess spirituality in our time. As a feminist theologian (or thealogian, as she puts it), Christ brings both knowledge and thoughtfulness to her reflections on her experience. The book is divided into two parts, "Dialogues with God and Tradition" and "Journey to the Goddess." This is an excellent read for anyone interested in the process of moving out of Christianity (or the other monotheistic traditions) into the embrace of the Mother.

Merlin Stone
When God Was a Woman: The Suppression of Women's Rites

An approach to Goddess spirituality more from a feminist than a magickal perspective, but of course the history covered and the conclusions reached are pretty much in alignment with how most Wiccans view the Goddess tradition. Stone celebrates the ancient faces of the Divine Feminine, and laments her defeat by the monotheistic religions. Like Leonard Shlain a generation later (see Chapter 27), she incisively points out the relationship between the suppression of Goddess spirituality and the suppression of women's freedom.

Janet and Stewart Farrar
The Witches' Goddess: The Feminine Principle of Divinity

Lots of practical information here for the neophyte or veteran Witch, this book includes three parts: "Discovering the Goddess," a survey of Goddess traditions from the dawn of time to the present; "Invoking the Goddess," a selection of rituals and magickal information on 13 Goddesses from various cultures (including Isis, Aradia, Demeter, and Persephone, among others), and "Goddesses of the World," an alphabetical listing of more than 1,000 Goddesses, famous and obscure. Like the Farrars' other books, this work carefully balances scholarship and practicality.

Raphael Patai
The Hebrew Goddess, Third enlarged edition

For everyone who thinks of the Jewish (and by extension, Christian) tradition as being monolithically and exclusively patriarchal. Patai uncovers hidden strands of polytheism and worship of the Divine Mother in the Hebrew tradition.

Kala Trobe
Invoke the Goddess: Visualization of Hindu, Greek, and Egyptian Deities

Approach the Goddess through ritual and visualizations. Trobe introduces you to 15 different guises of the Divine Feminine, with background information on the myths associated with each Goddess, along with practical advice on calling the Goddess in to your personal spiritual path.

Demetra George
Mysteries of the Dark Moon: The Healing Power of the Dark Goddess

The Goddess tradition regards the waxing and waning of the moon as a symbol of the rhythms of life; and just as the moon goes through her dark phase, so life has its winter times, its fallow times of rest, renewal, and healing. This book celebrates archetypes of the Dark Goddess and explores how she can be a force for rebirth and initiation in our lives.

Marija Gimbutas
The Language of the Goddess: Unearthing the Hidden Symbols of Western Civilization

Marija Gimbutas
The Civilization of the Goddess: The World of Old Europe

Two lavishly illustrated books that summarize the lifelong work of Gimbutas, a controversial European archaeologist who theorized that the prehistoric cultures of old Europe were egalitarian, non-violent, prosperous, and centered on Goddess worship. The massive amount of information contained in these two books serves not only as a brief tour through ancient Europe but also (and perhaps more importantly) as a source of inspiration for those who love the Goddess, and who wish to create a better world for today and tomorrow.

Barbara Ardinger, Ph.D.
Goddess Meditations

A variety of Goddess meditations, arranged by topic—so if you're trying to learn from past mistakes, meditate on White Buffalo Calf Woman, but if you're seeking healing, meditate on Coventina. One section features Goddess meditations for each of the chakras; another lists Goddesses associated with abstract principles (like learning, prosperity, or darkness).

The meditations themselves are brief (most are two to four pages long) forays into the magick of the interior world, where the seeker may encounter the Divine Feminine within the theater of the imagination.

Buffie Johnson
Lady of the Beasts: Ancient Images of the Goddess and Her Sacred Animals

From snakes to birds, from cows to deer, from dogs to horses, a wide array of animals have walked alongside the Goddess. With over three hundred images of Goddesses and their animal companions from throughout the world, this book celebrates the many faces of the Divine Feminine by celebrating the beasts who walk, swim, or fly at her side.

Monica Sjöö and Barbara Mor
The Great Cosmic Mother: Rediscovering the Religion of the Earth

An encyclopedic survey of the Goddess in history and her relationship to art, religion, spirituality, and most especially to women's bodies and to the earth. From the primacy of the Divine Mother in ancient times to the rise of patriarchy, culminating in a call to return to the ways of the Goddess. Sjöö is an artist, and her graceful Goddess images illuminate this book.

Jennifer Reif
Mysteries of Demeter: Rebirth of the Pagan Way

The story of Demeter and Persephone occupies a central place in classical myth, and many Wiccan traditions build their understanding of the sacred year around the drama of the mother who loses and regains her daughter. Reif, a Wiccan priestess, has developed an entire set of rituals, chants, prayers, and recipes for honoring the Great Mother in the guise of Demeter.

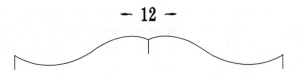

12

THE GOD
(AND MALE SPIRITUALITY)

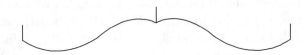

As with the Goddess, Wiccans have many different ways of thinking about and acknowledging the God of Wicca (known most often as the horned God or the Green Man). Among Dianic or feminist Witches, the God is often de-emphasized or omitted altogether. After all, since our culture has been overly focused on a male-only God for so many centuries now, a Wiccan tradition that focuses on a female-only Goddess is merely trying to bring a long overdue balance. However, most Wiccans acknowledge an appropriate role for the Divine Male in the Craft, with some taking pains to regard the Lord and the Lady as equals, while others see the Lady as taking prominence over her consort. As in so many aspects of Witchcraft, personal preference and coven tradition play an important role in determining just how prominent the God will be in any one person's practice.

In her book *The God of the Witches*, Margaret Murray suggests that the devil (whom accused witches during the European witch-hunts supposedly worshiped) was in fact the ancient God of the hunt or the forest, who in various cultures in Europe was depicted as having horns. Pan of the Greeks and Cernunnos of the Celts were but two forms of this primal masculine deity. In more recent years, many Witches have embraced the concept of the Green Man, based on an architectural motif found in many ancient churches and other buildings in Europe— a man's face covered with foliage, signifying the primal connection between the male principle of divinity and the surging life of the wildwoods.

In the literature of modern Wicca, the God often does not get as much attention as the Goddess. This is perhaps due to the fact that our culture remains under the massive influence of the God of Abraham—the God of Judaism, Christianity, and Islam. And since irrational fears of devil-worship linger in the minds of many who are misinformed about the benevolent nature of Wicca, the concept of the Horned One probably does not make for bestselling books! Still, the God is of vital importance to Wicca, if for no other reason than our culture's desperate need for healthy, positive models of masculinity.

While books on the God may be in short supply, some Pagan authors have explored the dynamics of masculinity, both in our culture as a whole as well as within the Wiccan world. Although many covens still have more women than men as members, Wicca is by no means a women's-only religion, and many men have found profound meaning in the mysteries of the Craft. Some of these men have written poetically of their experience as male Witches. Other books, like Jean Shinoda Bolen's *Gods in Every Man*, do not have any particular connection to the Craft, but nevertheless demonstrate the powerful role that mythical Gods can play in the lives of modern men.

Janet and Stewart Farrar
The Witches' God: Lord of the Dance

A companion to *The Witches' Goddess* (see Chapter 11), this book follows in much the same format as its feminine predecessor, a survey of God history (including a chapter on the grass widower that explores the implications of male monotheism, in which a God is worshiped without a corresponding Goddess), with a section on invoking Gods such as Pan, Osiris, Shiva, and Eros. The final section documents more than a thousand Gods from around the world, providing nuggets of information about how these figures can be honored by Wiccans.

William Anderson
Green Man: The Archetype of Our Oneness With the Earth

All over Europe, and most notably in many old churches, can be found carvings of the Green Man or the foliate head: a powerful masculine image of a face made of, or covered by, leaves and other foliage. This book, filled with photographs by Clive Hicks, celebrates the Green Man's history in art and architecture and speculates on how he represents a vestigial remnant of Pagan imagery as the masculine face of the Divine.

Teresa Moorey and Howard Moorey
Pagan Gods for Today's Man: A Beginner's Guide

Basic Pagan concepts of masculine divinity: Gods of wood and wild; the hunter, warrior, and hero; the trickster and the sacred fool; the Oak King and the Holly King. I think the book's title is unfortunate in that the Pagan God isn't just for men— just as men can benefit from the spirituality of the Goddess, women can benefit from an authentic and healthy spirituality of the God.

Patricia Merivale
Pan the Goat-God: His Myth in Modern Times
To Witches, Pan is one of the most distinct and striking of God-forms. But his popularity in modern times is not limited to practitioners of the old ways. This academic study by a Canadian professor of English Literature traces Pan's appearance in literary works over the past two centuries, from the Romantic poets up to the writing of D. H. Lawrence. This literary Pan is often a symbol of romanticism, of unrestrained sexuality and passion, of the wildness lurking at the edges of modern civilization.

John Williamson
The Oak King, The Holly King, and the Unicorn: The Myths and Symbols of the Unicorn Tapestries
This work of artistic and cultural history unravels the rich symbolism in the medieval Unicorn Tapestries housed at The Cloisters of the Metropolitan Museum of Art in New York City. Williamson shows how these 15th-century masterpieces have encoded within them the cosmology of pre-Christian Paganism— a ritual world-view based on Nature-oriented spirituality, in which the sacred hunt is essential for the regeneration, renewal, and survival of the people.

Alan Richardson
Earth God Rising: The Return of the Male Mysteries
Following the idea that all Gods are one God, this book weaves together the Green Man and the Horned One in a journey through Egypt, Camelot, the wilderness, and the ancient places of sacrifice, to find the powerful presence of the Divine Masculine in our own time, and in that God, to find a renewed way for men to relate lovingly toward the Goddess, toward women, and toward the land.

Nicholas R. Mann
The Dark God: A Personal Journey Through the Underworld

With echoes of *Midnight Express*, Mann's harrowing experience of 20 months in a Turkish prison inspired this meditation on the concept of the Dark God, challenging the God/Devil duality held by mainstream culture and replacing it with a much more useful quaternity of the God, the Goddess, the Dark Goddess, and the Dark God. The author explores how honoring and accepting the Dark God (and Goddess) can help us release and transform the human capacity for violence and evil.

Eric L. Fitch
In Search of Herne the Hunter

Nigel Jackson
Masks of Misrule: The Horned God and His Cult in Europe

Two British books which explore the native mythic and folkloric traditions related to the masculine dimension of Pagan spirituality. Fitch explores the history and lore surrounding Herne (a British variation of the Celtic horned God Cernunnos, who in folklore became to hunting what Robin Hood is to social justice), while Jackson considers the Horned God traditions not only in relation to hunting, but also as an agricultural and trickster God.

R. J. Stewart
Celebrating the Male Mysteries

This attempt to codify the mystery element of male spirituality into a user-friendly modern system draws on Kabbalistic, Pagan, shamanic, and psychological sources. The book is designed to be used by anyone with an interest in the topic, even those without a background in metaphysics or magick. By exploring the relationship between men and the Goddess, the five branches of male experience including the warrior, prophet, poet, priest, and king, and through introductory exercises in such areas as fostering innerworld contact, this book serves masculine spirituality both as an ancient tradition, and as a renewed tradition for today.

Jean Shinoda Bolen, M.D.
Gods in Every Man: A New Psychology of Men's Lives and Loves

One wonderful reason why ancient myths of Gods (and Goddesses) can be so helpful to spiritual seekers today is how the different personalities of the deities can teach us about our own souls. This book, the sequel to Bolen's bestseller *Goddesses in Everywoman*, examines such Gods as Zeus, Poseidon, Hades, Apollo, Hermes, and Dionysus, exploring how understanding the Gods is a direct path to understanding the psychology of men.

Kerr Cuhulain
Wiccan Warrior: Walking a Spiritual Path in a Sometimes Hostile World

While not written exclusively for men, this book calls for a renaissance of the Warrior archetype among Pagans—an archetype historically associated with men. The true Warrior does not wantonly wage battle, but rests secure in his own power to defend all he loves. Our world, where Pagans sometimes are denied civil rights and where the sacred land is defiled in the name of profit, needs healthy and balanced warriors.

A.J. Drew
Wicca Spellcraft for Men: A Spellbook for Male Pagans

The author leads off this book by declaring "Wicca is not a fashion statement." Hooray! This straightforward guide to magickal work, filled with numerous recipes and lore, was written specifically with men in mind.

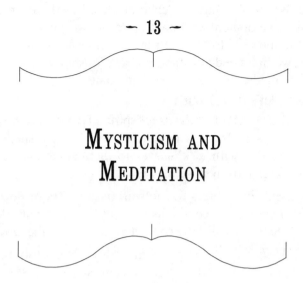

Mysticism and Meditation

Our journey through the elements of Wicca began by recognizing the central role that the Goddess and the God—the Lord and the Lady—play in the spirituality of the Craft. But now we need to consider: what is spirituality? After all, the common stereotype of Witchcraft involves casting spells and working magick, activities which may or may not have a spiritual component to them at all. If a person is casting a spell to get a better paying job or to lose weight and be more sexually attractive, can such endeavors truly be labeled spiritual?

Actually, most Witches would say yes. Part of the beauty of Wicca lies in how it's okay to want more money, abundance, health, and sex in our lives, and as long as we refrain from harming others, it's okay to work spells to attain such goals. But Wicca is far, far more than a system of wish-fulfillment. Indeed, most Wiccan elders would insist that the spiritual aspect of Wicca takes priority over the magickal aspect.

Which is why I've put this chapter ahead of the chapters on psychic development and magick. Before we can ask the Goddess and the God to bless our lives with whatever it is that we desire, we first need to establish a relationship with them. This is where meditation and mysticism come in.

First, let's define our terms:

- *Magick* involves the use of spiritual power to achieve one's goals (see Chapter 16). Incidentally, spelling magick with a 'k' serves to distinguish spiritual magick from stage magic.

- *Mysticism* refers to the spiritual process of developing higher consciousness—in Wiccan terms, this means establishing contact or union with the Gods.

- *Meditation* is the art of inner listening, a tool that nearly all spiritual traditions insist is the first step toward developing mystical consciousness.

Because magick involves spiritual power, aspiring magicians need to start by developing their spirituality—by studying mysticism and practicing meditation. As we develop spiritually, we become more capable of using magick in powerful and responsible ways.

The books in this section can help Witches to learn the basics of the spiritual life. While some of these books are explicitly magickal or occult-oriented, others have a much broader spiritual focus, or even represent mainstream religious traditions such as Buddhism or Christianity. After all, mysticism and magick transcend religious boundaries—they are universal human experiences, available to people of all spiritual paths. Of course, some of the theological ideas in a book on non-Wiccan mysticism may not be something a Witch would agree with, but the underlying principles of spirituality can still help Witches to foster inner growth.

Geoffrey Parrinder
Mysticism in the World's Religions

Wayne Teasdale
The Mystic Heart: Discovering a Universal Spirituality in the World's Religions

While many books on mystical spirituality approach the inner life from the perspective of one particular religious or philosophical position, these books take the larger view—considering the universal elements of mysticism found in traditions the world over. Parrinder's book reads more like a textbook, analyzing the similarities and differences of the various flavors of world mysticism. Teasdale approaches the topic from more of an experiential basis, drawing on his experience as a Catholic monk who has integrated elements of Hinduism into his spiritual practice.

Ram Dass
Be Here Now

A classic text of hippie spirituality first published in 1971, written by an early LSD researcher who went to India and became a devotee of eastern mysticism. Ram Dass has gone on to become one of the West's most articulate and beloved spokesmen for universal spirituality. This book playfully explores the maze of human consciousness, using Hindu concepts to snap the minds of its western readers into wakefulness. Wiccans will particularly love how it honors the Divine Mother (whether portrayed as a sexy Eve, complete with her apple, or as the fearsome Kali, with a necklace of skulls and her tongue dripping blood).

Carl McColman
The Aspiring Mystic: Practical Steps for Spiritual Seekers

I was hesitant to endorse a book that I myself wrote, but my friend Francesca De Grandis insisted it be included. She told me that if I couldn't endorse my own book, I should let her do it. So here's what she had to say: "*The Aspiring Mystic* is a serious text about mysticism. If Goddess spirituality is going to remain vital and relevant, it must stay in the hands of its practitioners. This book helps people claim, be empowered by, and revel in, their own experience with the other realms."

Matthew Fox
Whee! We, Wee All the Way Home...A Guide to the New Sensual Spirituality

Matthew Fox is the Catholic priest who got into trouble with his superiors because he hired Starhawk to teach at his Spirituality Institute (he eventually left the Catholic Church and became an Episcopal priest). This book explores the role of ecstasy (real, juicy, orgasmic ecstasy) in the mystical life. While it is Christian in tone, its vision is radical enough that most Witches should find it informative and inspiring.

Galen Gillotte
Book of Hours: Prayers to the Goddess

Here's the closest thing yet to a Wiccan prayer book. Daily devotions for morning, evening, and night, along with seasonal and lunar observances, make this a perfect book for anyone who wants to exercise a daily devotion centered on the Goddess. Gillotte, who is a solitary Witch, has done the Wiccan community a service by providing this text as one possible way to weave Goddess devotion into everyday life.

Gill Edwards
Pure Bliss: The Art of Living in Soft Time

New Age mysticism from a popular British author who explores how cultivating a spiritual practice can bring joy into life. Her concept of "soft time" (basically, surrendering the ego-driven need to be in control, so that time—and life—seem to flow effortlessly) is not only a core mystical principle, but also a principle similar to what Wiccans know as "perfect love and perfect trust."

Caitlín and John Matthews
The Western Way: A Practical Guide to the Western Mystery Tradition

Dolores Ashcroft-Nowicki
Highways of the Mind: The Art and History of Pathworking

These are two books that could have easily been profiled in several different chapters: the Matthewses and Ashcroft-Nowicki are respected magickal authors, and these books combine mystical spirituality with magickal imagery, all based on the Western occult tradition. I decided to emphasize them as mystical books because I believe they demonstrate the link between mysticism and magick: magickal practice begins with disciplines like guided visualization, pathworking (a form of visualization), and meditation. These books are truly essential, for they not only will help you develop your mystical spirituality, but they will do so within a symbolic and traditional context that is very much Pagan- and Wiccan-friendly.

Joan Budilovsky and Eve Adamson
The Complete Idiot's Guide to Meditation

The Complete Idiot's books are designed to present basic information in an easy-to-use format—and this volume delivers the goods. I wish the title said "beginner" instead of "idiot," because this book, like others in its series, is an excellent guide for the absolute novice. The authors describe how meditation provides not only spiritual, but also health benefits, and offer helpful suggestions on how to establish a regular meditation practice.

Lawrence LeShan
How to Meditate: A Guide to Self-Discovery

This classic introduction to meditation, written by a respected psychotherapist, considers the dynamics of the inner life from a psychological, rather than religious, perspective. LeShan examines both the mental and physiological effects of meditation, and points out some of the more common pitfalls to avoid. Includes instructions on how to practice several different styles of meditation.

Linda Johnson
Meditation is Boring? Putting Life into Your Spiritual Practice

An honest book about taking your meditation practice to a deeper level. It's written from the perspective of a yoga practitioner but has enough universal appeal to be helpful to the average Witch.

Jon Kabat-Zinn
Wherever You Go, There You Are: Mindfulness Meditation in Everyday Life

A bestselling book about the application of Buddhist principles of mindfulness to the raw material of ordinary life. The application to Wicca is easy to see: Witches regard all things as sacred, and therefore resist the idea that one must run off to a monastery or ashram to be spiritual. Mindfulness is about paying attention, which is a prerequisite to seeing the movement of the Gods in the natural world.

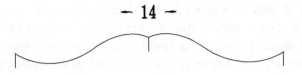

14

SHAMANISM

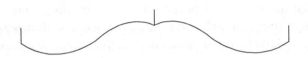

In his book *Ecstasies: Deciphering the Witches' Sabbat* (profiled in Chapter 27), Italian historian Carlo Ginzburg suggests that when the authorities attempted to stamp out Witchcraft during the burning times, what they were actually attacking was the last remnants of the ancient shamanistic spirituality of pre-Christian Europe. His theory makes sense, for modern Wicca, as a spiritual system, combines mystical and meditative spirituality with the earthy, primal practices of shamanism (the spiritual practices of healing, ritual, and spirit contact found in tribal and indigenous cultures throughout the world).

By themselves, meditation and mysticism can leave spiritual seekers too stuck in their heads. While meditating, it's easy to get lost in the dramas of our thoughts and states of mental awareness. As a doorway to higher consciousness, mysticism sometimes seems to be unconcerned with the needs of the body.

Meditation and mysticism often function like computers—they can give the mind a workout while leaving the rest of the body stiff from sitting still so long.

Wiccan spirituality seeks balance; therefore, the heady, mental disciplines of mysticism and meditation need to be balanced by the earthy, embodied, and even erotic traditions of Nature-oriented and shamanic forms of spirituality. Shamanism encompasses the great traditions of indigenous and tribal-based spirituality, such as the Lakota medicine man (or woman) or the Yoruba healer. Shamanism is the primal spirituality of the natural world.

Shamanic spirituality explores both inner and outer dimensions of the wilderness beyond the scope of human influence. Through spirit contact, rituals involving totems (or power animals), and the lore associated with sacred plants, animals, and stones, these primal forms of spirituality bring healing and wisdom to its practitioners.

Today, shamanism is not just for tribal or indigenous people; thanks to a number of Western visionaries such as Michael Harner, Mircea Eliade, and Terence McKenna, the core principles and practices of shamanic spirituality are available even to urban dwellers in the industrialized nations. This "core shamanism" often lacks the deep rootedness that indigenous people bring to the spiritual identity, but that's not so much the fault of the spirituality as it is a commentary on the rootless culture we inhabit. Perhaps when we take the time to create and nurture meaningful communities in our lives, our spiritual practice—even something like core shamanism, which is basically a method of borrowing spirituality from other cultures—will develop its own rootedness.

Indeed, this is part of the magick of Wicca. The key elements of core shamanism—spirit contact, ritual, the magickal use of plants, animals, and minerals—all appear within Wiccan practice. Within Wicca, those who are drawn to shamanism can find a spiritual center that has its own deep roots, without relying on borrowing from the ways of indigenous peoples, many of whom resent how people of European ancestry take without asking (even when what is being taken are spiritual practices).

Each of the following books either celebrates an aspect of shamanism, or highlights the shamanic dimension of Wicca or points out some other aspect of spirituality deeply grounded in Nature. Because Wicca is a Nature spirituality, anything that can help us stay mindful of our primal Nature connection supports our path.

Mircea Eliade
Shamanism: Archaic Techniques of Ecstasy

The granddaddy of shamanism books, this is an academic study of the subject by one of the 20th century's premier religious scholars. This is *not* how to be a shaman in 10 easy lessons, but rather a serious and thorough study of shamanism and other primal/tribal spiritual practices the world over. Here is the scholarly documentation of such core shamanic practices as initiation, drumming, spirit contact, and healing.

Michael Harner
The Way of the Shaman, updated edition

First published in 1980, this book became a classic introduction of core shamanic spiritual practices for the western reader. Harner liberates shamanism from the confines of the ivory tower, combining theory with case studies and exercises suitable for group or individual use. After writing the book, the author went on to found the Institute for Shamanic Studies, and many more western shamanic practitioners of varying pedigree and ability followed in his wake.

Tom Cowan
Fire in the Head: Shamanism and the Celtic Spirit
Tom Cowan
Shamanism as a Spiritual Practice for Daily Life

Cowan presents shamanic spirituality as a core practice available to urban dwellers. His books explain the universal elements of the shamanic way and how those elements can be incorporated into modern life. From vision questing to the use of power animals and spirit teachers in the quest for wisdom and healing power, Cowan's guidance makes shamanism accessible. While *Shamanism as a Spiritual Practice* is not a cultural-specific study, *Fire in the Head* considers the shamanic nature of ancient Celtic traditions and explores their relevance to the modern seeker.

Olga Kharitidi, M.D.
Entering the Circle: Ancient Secrets of Siberian Wisdom Discovered by a Russian Psychiatrist

A first-person account of how shamanic wisdom can transform the practice of western healing practices, this time told through the experience of a Soviet doctor whose frustration with working in the confines of the communist medical community was transformed by her encounter with indigenous healers in the mountains of Siberia.

John Perkins
Shape Shifting: Shamanic Techniques for Global and Personal Transformation

Americans love to pay lip service to transformation as a life goal; yet shamanic practitioners from around the globe have practiced the transformational skills of shapeshifting for thousands of years. Shapeshifting can be a way of relating to the natural world, of honoring a hunter's prey, of healing the sick, and of transforming entire communities. Perkins draws on his experience studying with shamans the world over, to present the theory and practice of shapeshifting for seekers in the post-industrial world.

John Perkins
The World is as You Dream It: Shamanic Teachings From the Amazon and Andes

Deep in the rain forest and high in the mountains of South America, native shamans continue to practice their healing arts. Perkins not only has traveled throughout the region, he has led tours of North American doctors and scientists who have gone with him to learn the wisdom of the shaman. Among other things, he recounts the powerful role of the dream in indigenous spirituality.

Gabrielle Roth with John Loudon
Maps to Ecstasy: A Healing Journey for the Untamed Spirit

Gabrielle Roth
Sweat Your Prayers: Movement as Spiritual Practice

The vision of Gabrielle Roth, who combines artistic magick as musician and dancer with her practice as a shaman and writer, is one that body-positive Pagans can readily accept. *Maps to Ecstasy* explores the landscape of the urban shaman through the five sacred powers of being, loving, knowing, seeing, and healing. This is a shamanism that transforms life into art, and art into healing. In *Sweat Your Prayers*, she presents dance and rhythm as powerful teachers; through five universal rhythms, including flowing, staccato, chaos, lyrical, and stillness, we can free our bodies, clear our minds, and express our spiritual yearning in a complete and holistic way.

Sandra Ingerman
Soul Retrieval: Mending the Fragmented Self

Focussing on one element of core shamanism—the practice of retrieving fragments or parts of the soul that have been lost, thereby healing a person of disease that is seen to be related to soul fragmentation. As a healer, the shaman takes on the task of journeying through the spirit world in search of a person's lost soul fragments, and retrieving those soul bits as a part of the person's healing process.

Ted Andrews
Animal-Speak: The Spiritual & Magical Powers of Creatures Great & Small

A wonderful reference book compiling the lore, legend, and magickal powers associated with more than a hundred different animals. If animals come to you in dreams or meditations, or if you feel drawn to a particular animal as your totem or power animal, this book can provide insight into the lessons and gifts that particular animal may bring you.

Nathaniel Altman
The Deva Handbook: How to Work with Nature's Subtle Energies

Call them devas, Fairies, or simply Nature spirits, wisdom traditions from the world over teach us how to connect and work with the powers of the land. This book not only presents the basics of devic contact, but considers real world examples of places where such contact has long been established.

Robert Lawlor
Voices of the First Day: Awakening in the Aboriginal Dreamtime

Shamanism from down under; a lavishly illustrated celebration of the indigenous Australian people and their culture. Out of the Dreamtime came all things—including a culture that lived in harmony with the earth for tens of thousands of years, until the white Europeans showed up and nearly killed them all off. Lawlor considers many aspects of aboriginal wisdom, including myths, social practices, rituals, and initiatory customs.

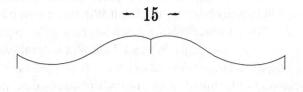

15

Psychic
Development

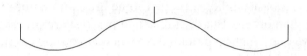

What do mysticism, meditation, and shamanism share in common? Each embodies a different quality or form of psychic experience.

Deriving from the Greek word for mind (psyche), the concept of the psychic encompasses the totality of mental/spiritual experience—including the ability to access wisdom, knowledge, and experience beyond what is normally possible within the limited experience of having a body in space and time. Psychic ability enables a person to receive guidance, inspiration, and information from sources beyond her or his own mind and body. Such a source could include one's higher self, spirit guides, Fairy contacts, angels, deities, extraterrestrial beings, or those who have died.

Wiccans vary widely in their view of the role psychic phenomena should play in the Craft. For many, such transcendental guidance is regarded as an essential feature of magickal spirituality.

Others see it as less important than personal empowerment or skills such as herbal healing. While all Witches are free to possess or develop psychic skill, one need not be a gifted psychic in order to be an accomplished Wiccan. I know of several Wiccans, one of whom is a High Priestess of a large coven, who are gifted leaders, teachers, and ritualists, but who humbly disclaim any particular psychic gift. Of course, I think these Witches are more psychic than they admit. My point: Even if you don't think you possess psychic skill or are not particularly interested in it, you still could find much meaningful experience as a practitioner of the Craft.

In many ways, psychic power is like athletic prowess. Everyone has a basic ability, although some are more naturally talented than others. But discipline and practice are necessary to achieve one's highest potential. So whether your psychic ability involves a clear ability to communicate with spirits, a powerful gift of clairvoyance or clairaudience, or merely a humble tendency to feel hunches that always turn out to be dead right; with an open mind and a willingness to put forth effort, you should be able to strengthen and hone your skills.

Most of the books profiled in this chapter involve teaching ways to develop and strengthen your psychic ability. Some of these books provide background information in psychic studies as well—helpful especially for those who have a naturally skeptical mind. Sad to say, the realm of the psychic has always attracted an element of fraudulence and chicanery, which is why I've also included Joanne D. S. McMahon's and Anna M. Lascurain's *Shopping For Miracles*—a helpful book on what to expect from a professional psychic, which points out the distinctions between authentic psychic readings and, well, humbuggery.

Psychic phenomena make for an endlessly fascinating field of study. Like so many other aspects of Wicca, this is something that should not only be studied, but experienced. Learning to access your own connection to higher guidance can be an empowering journey. As these books demonstrate, there's no one right way to go about this. When pursuing psychic development, follow the advice of any true psychic: trust your intuition.

Marcia L. Pickands
Psychic Abilities: How to Train and Use Them

Using Tarot and numerology as doorways to the mysteries of the mind, this book examines the difference between psychic readings and divination, ethical considerations of psychic ability, and the most awesome of psychic skills—the ability to communicate with the dead. The author explains the difference between spirituality and psychic ability, showing why psychics need to be spiritually grounded.

Diane Stein
All Women Are Psychics

An affirming and encouraging book for women who have had their intuitive ability suppressed or discounted by the dominant culture in which we live. Along with giving a basic overview of the varieties of psychic experience, Stein recounts the life stories of dozens of psychic women to illustrate how available psychic ability is to the ordinary person.

Shakti Gawain
Creative Visualization: Use the Power of Your Imagination to Create What You Want in Life, Revised edition

One of the classics of contemporary spirituality, this deceptively simple book introduces the reader to one of the most basic of psychic (and by extension, magickal) principles: using the power of the mind to create or shape reality by visualizing a desired goal or outcome.

Ted Andrews
How to Meet and Work with Spirit Guides

Mike Samuels, M.D. and Hal Bennett
Spirit Guides: Access to Inner Worlds

These are both tiny little books, the kind that avid readers can devour in a single sitting. And so, they appear deceptively simple in their discussion of spirit contact. Samuels and Bennett take a psychological approach, and may appeal to people who are naturally skeptical by nature; Andrews takes a more esoteric approach that will appeal to those with an established interest in occult philosophy. But what both books share is their enthusiasm for a simple process of accessing spiritual guidance through interior journeying. Whether you are by nature a skeptic or a believer, these books can show you practical ways to contact and learn from your own spiritual allies.

Edgar Cayce
Auras: An Essay on the Meaning of Colors (booklet)

Ted Andrews
How to See and Read the Aura

W. E. Butler
How to Read the Aura and Practice Psychometry, Telepathy, and Clairvoyance

Each of these books provides basic insight into the nature of the energy field that surrounds the human body, known as the aura. From the halo of Christian art to the astral body as experienced by spiritualists, the aura has long been recognized by mystics and metaphysicians as an integral part of the Mind/Body/Spirit complex. Seeing or reading auras is a basic psychic skill, for the aura provides information through color and vibration regarding the individual's mental, emotional, and psychic state of mind. Cayce's essay, written shortly before his death, is valuable if for no other reason than the fact that he was not a prolific writer and left behind few of his own words. Butler's and Andrew's books are more contemporary approaches to the art of sensing and working with the auras, and incorporating aura reading into an overall process of psychic development.

Tom Graves
The Diviner's Handbook: Your Guide to Divining Anything From Lost Objects, Precious Metals to the Mysteries of Your Own Mind

I still remember my friends in rural, backwoods (and heavily Baptist) Tennessee who hired a "water-witch" to help them locate the site for a well on their new property. The diviner came out, made his recommendation, and once the well was drilled, the water flowed plentifully. That folks in a rural, largely-Christian area would call a diviner a "water-witch" clearly reveals the powerful connection between the Craft and psychic systems of decision making. Divining involves far more than using a Y-shaped stick to find underground water. Most diviners use pendulums or angle rods (two L-shaped wire rods, one held in each hand) to assist them in accessing the wisdom that resides deep within the mysteries of their mind. What makes the pendulum swirl or the angle rods twitch is, ultimately, the psychic skill of the person holding the tool. Grave's book, filled with background information and helpful exercises, can help the novice diviner develop her or his skills.

Mona Lisa Schulz, M.D., Ph.D.
Awakening Intuition: Using Your Mind-Body Network for Insight and Healing

For Witches with an academic or scholarly background, many of the books on psychic development may seem overly simplistic.

Such educated Witches will welcome Mona Lisa Schulz's intelligent and thorough discussion of intuition. Her primary focus is on developing one's intuition for the purpose of understanding the mind-body connection and fostering one's own health and well-being. This process of developing intuition provides a solid foundation for further psychic development.

Robert A. Monroe
Journeys Out of the Body
The story of an ordinary businessman who began to undergo experiences of leaving his physical body behind and travelling via the astral body. Such experiences led to a careful study of human consciousness and psychic abilities, resulting not only in this book, but also in the founding of the Monroe Institute, an organization dedicated to the study of out-of-body experiences and the mechanics of human consciousness.

Joanne D. S. McMahon, Ph.D. and Anna M. Lascurain, Esq.
Shopping For Miracles: A Guide to Psychics & Psychic Powers
Not a book on psychic development, but rather a consumer guide to professional psychics. What to expect from a psychic, what to watch out for (the section on psychic scoundrels is quite illuminating), and some basic advice on developing your own psychic skills. I think anyone who is thinking about becoming a professional psychic should read this book, taking seriously its call for ethics and accountability.

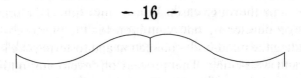

16

MAGICK

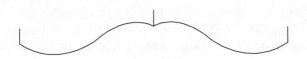

The topics covered in the last three chapters—mysticism, shamanism, and psychic development—pave the way for magick, one of the most central (and misunderstood) elements of Wiccan spirituality.

Many spiritual writers have assumed that magick and mysticism are somehow opposed to one another (see Evelyn Underhill's *Mysticism*, which includes a chapter that makes precisely this assertion). But Wiccans, who understand both yin (receptive) and yang (assertive) energies are necessary elements of existence, see magick and mysticism as equally necessary to create a holistic and balanced spiritual life. Mysticism involves opening up the heart and soul to receive experiences of divine ecstasy and union with God(dess) through disciplines like meditation. Magick, by contrast, involves exercising the will to shape mental or psychic forces to achieve desired results, on either the spiritual or physical plane. Mysticism involves love and trust; magick involves will and power. We need the open, spacious, ego-lessening experience of meditation to keep us balanced, humble, and down to earth. We also need magick, the key to dancing with the divine love and power of the Gods, to create positive change in our lives. A person who is mystical, but not magickal, is spiritually passive—a metaphysical doormat. But a person who is magickal with no mystical dimension is equally out of balance, hungry for power but unconcerned with love. Such magick without love isn't afraid to harm others to get its own way. This, emphatically, is *not* the way of Wicca.

The books profiled in this chapter cover a wide terrain. Some provide scientific or spiritual theories of the nature and laws of magick, explaining what it is and how and why it works. But other titles have a more practical, down-to-earth orientation. These are the books that explain how to do it.

I must admit, I'm rather biased against spell cookbooks— anthologies of spells for every purpose, with detailed instructions on how to achieve this or that desired goal. Sure, some of the titles I've profiled, both here and in other chapters, do contain spells for you to try. But I believe spells are best learned from a teacher, not a book. This is because spellcraft, unlike cooking, involves far more than just mixing up some ingredients and turning up the heat. Meditation, concentration, timing, and a positive working relationship with your spirit guides all play critical roles in magick. Books can provide lots of information, but experience is ultimately the only way to learn these things. And with a qualified teacher, your trial-and-error curve will be dramatically reduced. Meanwhile, before diving into the spell cookbooks, I recommend taking the time to learn the principles of magick (read Janet and Stewart Farrar's *Spells and How They Work* to master these principles). Also brush up on your ethics—read Robin Wood's *When, Why, If* (profiled in Chapter 8). Then you will be less at risk for shooting blind with your spells. Here's an old principle that magickal adepts teach their students: "Never conjure up anything you don't have the power to banish." Before doing a spell, be sure you know what you're doing. If in doubt, put down the book and find a competent Wiccan elder to teach you. Studying with an elder requires patience and dedication, but in the long run you'll be the better Witch for it.

Amber K
True Magick: A Beginner's Guide
The absolute basics. Suitable for the beginner who wants the bottom-line fundamentals spelled out. Amber K is a respected leader in the Craft community, and her understanding of magick and its role within the old religion falls squarely in the Wiccan mainstream.

Doreen Valiente
Natural Magic
Written by one of the founding mothers of the modern Craft, this is a basic introduction to the natural (as opposed to ceremonial) tradition of magick and how it can be applied today. Topics covered include the four Elements, herbs, numbers, colors, talismans and amulets, dreams, sex, and weather.

Isaac Bonewits
Real Magic: An Introductory Treatise on the Basic Principles of Yellow Magic, Revised edition
Bonewits, the articulate and outspoken founder of the Druid organization Ár nDraíocht Féin, is probably the only person ever to have received a degree in Magic from an institute of higher learning (U.C. Berkeley). The intelligent tone of this book reflects its academic origins. It explores the laws of magick, parapsychology, rituals, spells, and various other topics related to occult phenomena.

Louis Pauwels and Jacques Bergier
The Morning of the Magicians

David Carroll and Barry Saxe
Natural Magic: The Magical State of Being

Two classic books on the reality and plausibility of magick, written especially for the skeptical (but open-minded) inquirer. *The Morning of the Magicians* was an occult bestseller in the 1960s; it explores magick as a doorway to higher consciousness. *Natural Magic*, although not as comprehensive, covers similar material.

Shekhinah Mountainwater
Ariadne's Thread: A Workbook of Goddess Magic

Many books on magick are written from a traditionalist perspective of depicting the Divine as a male-only God. This exploration of the feminine/Goddess-oriented dimension of magick is therefore especially Wiccan-friendly. Organized around themes of gathering, spinning, and weaving, this book considers how magick functions to reconnect women with the Goddess, women with their bodies and the land, and women with their own power.

David Spangler
Everyday Miracles: The Inner Art of Manifestation

Spangler describes himself as a freelance mystic, meaning his spiritual orientation is universalist in nature—this is not a textbook of specifically Wiccan or Pagan magick. But the concept of manifestation is central to any type of practical magick, and this book provides a general introduction to the spiritual procedures involved in making things happen, revealing how it is ultimately not so much about making things happen, but about living in alignment with the creativity and abundance flowing throughout the universe.

Lilith McLelland
Spellcraft: A Primer for the Young Magician

More and more teenagers and children feel drawn to the world of magick and Wicca; often, such youngsters don't have a teacher or elder to guide them in the ways of responsible and ethical spellwork. This book provides, without condescension, a safe introduction to the magickal arts for kids of all ages (yes, I know adults who swear by this book).

Patricia Telesco
Exploring Candle Magick: Candle Spells, Charms, Rituals, and Divinations

Candles play a central role in most forms of Western magick, whether to symbolize an external force (like a God or a Goddess) or to serve as a focus for the magickal intention of the spell being performed. Telesco provides basic information on color, scent, ritual, and other elements of using candles effectively in your magickal work.

Itzhak Bentov
Stalking the Wild Pendulum: On the Mechanics of Consciousness

According to Dion Fortune, magick is "the art of changing consciousness at will." But this goes beyond the mere ability to achieve the deep alpha and theta states that practitioners of meditation attain. Magick changes consciousness to change the relationship between our consciousness and our environment. This is why real magick has results not only on a person's mind and attitude, but on the physical circumstances of her or his life as well. This scientific odyssey through consciousness provides a useful overview to those who want to understand the physics of magick.

Janet and Stewart Farrar
Spells and How They Work

Why are spells effective? What is the practical application of psychic ability? These are the questions that the Farrars explore in this book, which not only dissects the concept of the spell, but also provides a historical survey of spellcraft from around the world. The book includes charts of planetary hours, planetary squares, and magickal alphabets.

Barbara Sher
Wishcraft: How to Get What You Really Want

Timothy Miller, Ph.D.
How to Want What You Have: Discovering the Magic and Grandeur of Ordinary Existence

Some people are good at magick but lousy at life. Such magickal people, with occult knowledge to burn, actually lead unhappy lives that they feel powerless to change, or dull their minds with substance abuse or other self-sabotaging behaviors. It's as if they put so much energy into esoterica that they have nothing left over for making their real-world dreams come true. In becoming a Witch, don't make the mistake of getting so enthralled by spells and rituals that you allow your mundane life to be a mess. These books, about getting your life in order, are not magickal in any occult sense, but can inspire you to use magick where it matters most: in creating a happy, fulfilling, successful life. Barbara Sher provides a practical roadmap for setting and achieving goals, while Timothy Miller suggests we define life not in terms of what we want, but in terms of the blessings we already have. Master the principles in these two books, and then your magick will flow with power and authority.

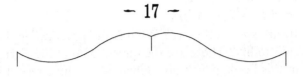

17

DIVINATION

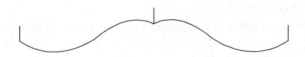

Because Wicca is the Craft of the Wise, to be a Witch means to be a wise woman or man. Wisdom is different from knowledge: knowledge involves merely the gross accumulation of facts. But wisdom requires the ability to discern meaning out of what is known. A knowledgeable person might be able to tell you how many cars are being manufactured each year in the United States, while a wise person will speak to the impact of emissions on the environment.

To attain the wisdom of Wicca, the student of the Craft needs to master knowledge of both spiritual as well as mundane matters. A Witch knows the ways of the Goddess and the God and also understands basic spiritual principles— which are not unique to Wicca, but which truly embody the spiritual knowledge of cultures the world over. But Witchcraft is more than just some sort of abstract, esoteric exercise in mystical concepts. Truly wise Witches possess as much knowledge about herbalism as about reincarnation; as much about natural foods as about mythology; and as much about managing stress as about casting spells. Wicca does not discriminate between spiritual and material aspects of life. All aspects of life are sacred to the God and the Goddess; therefore, a truly accomplished Witch will demonstrate wisdom in many ways, both magickal and mundane.

Divination beautifully integrates the spiritual and material dimensions of life. Simply put, divination involves the use of one or more tools to access divine wisdom—wisdom that may be applied to practical concerns. Divinatory tools such as Tarot or astrology help people open their souls to receive divine wisdom. Such wisdom often surfaces from a person's own deep subconscious (which is why the interpretation of dreams also functions as a method of divination). Divine wisdom may also be encountered through the rich symbolism of the cards or the stars—symbolism that contains the acquired wisdom of generations of spiritual seekers and masters who have gone before us. Divination tools may also serve as psychic doorways through which our intuition may receive information from guides and spirits.

Divination is practical, but it's important not to expect too little out of these tools. While there's nothing wrong with using divination to ask questions about one's day-to-day existence, don't forget that at the hands of a gifted Witch, these tools have power far beyond mere fortune telling. The wisdom revealed through a majestic tool such as the Tarot or the I Ching will tell you far more about your life than merely whether your boyfriend really loves you or whether you'll get that raise. It is the wisdom of the soul, the wisdom of union with the Lord and the Lady. It is the wisdom of deep inner knowing and self-empowerment that speaks to our soul purpose and mission in life. The treasures to be found in the cards or the stars have the potential to bring far more happiness than a mere paycheck or phone call ever could.

Dreams

Ann Faraday, Ph.D.
The Dream Game

One of my favorite dream books. Instead of merely listing a dictionary of symbols with possible interpretations, this book combines psychological and parapsychological insight in its exploration of the wondrous landscape of the dreaming world. Indeed, Faraday argues against the concept of dream dictionaries altogether, instead leading the reader through common dream themes (flying, nudity, sex, finding or losing money, and so forth) to help the reader learn to interpret dreams intuitively. Unafraid of the mystical dimension of dreaming, Faraday devotes attention to lucid dreaming and the relationship between dreams and out-of-body experiences.

Karri Allrich
A Witch's Book of Dreams: Understanding the Power of Dreams & Symbols

Like Ann Faraday, I'm not a big fan of dream dictionaries. But this one was developed specifically for Witches, and Allrich states clearly that no one interpretation of a symbol can be absolute. Her dream dictionary is meant to encourage and inspire you to develop your own. This book also has helpful introductory material on archetypes, symbols, and the importance of the shadow and the nightmare in dreamwork.

Astrology

Joanna Martine Woolfolk
The Only Astrology Book You'll Ever Need

Astrology is a complex discipline, in which planets, constellations, and houses (positions in the sky) all have meaning. Like I said in Chapter 4, a person could devote his or her entire life's metaphysical work to astrology—and for that matter, fill their library with books on the subject. So this book's title seems a bit on the pompous side. Nevertheless, this really is an excellent one-volume introduction to astrology; providing enough basics to cast, and interpret, your natal horoscope.

Caroline W. Casey
Making the Gods Work for You: the Astrological Language of the Psyche

Forget everything your high school physics teacher told you about astrology being a silly hobby for flaky people. Casey brings an intelligent sophistication to her work, and in this introduction to the symbolic language of the planets and stars, she demonstrates just how intellectually viable astrology can be. She combines her work as a guide for the soul with a balanced sense of political activism, showing how the language of the soul can inspire us to work for a better world.

Tarot

Mary K. Greer
Tarot For Your Self: A Workbook for Personal Transformation

Studying the Tarot can seem daunting, with its 78 images and rich storehouse of esoteric symbolism. Greer begins with a beautifully simple premise: To learn the magick and mystery of the cards, begin by using them as a tool for personal spiritual growth. This book includes all the normal this-card-means-that verbiage, but mostly consists of a series of exercises for using the cards in meditation, self-discovery, personal planning, decision-making, and other useful applications. Doing these exercises makes the intimidation factor melt away, so that using the cards (whether reading for self or others) becomes a true joy.

Rachel Pollack
Seventy-Eight Degrees of Wisdom: A Book of Tarot
Profound and detailed exploration of the symbolism and divinatory meanings of each card in the Rider-Waite-Smith Tarot. If you've wondered why there are Hebrew letters on the Wheel of Fortune card or why the pillars behind the Priestess have a B and a J on them, read this book. Pollack's detailed and articulate descriptions of the cards and their esoteric meanings make the imagery of the Tarot come alive.

The runes and other sacred alphabets

Nigel Pennick
Magical Alphabets
Alphabets have a long history of use in magickal and divinatory ways, and at least two European alphabets (the runes and the Celtic ogham) are used as divination tools today. Pennick considers esoteric uses of the runes, the ogham, the Greek and Hebrew alphabets, and also looks at the importance of letters in alchemy, talismans, and magickal squares.

Edred Thorsson
Futhark: A Handbook of Rune Magic
An introduction to the history, lore, and magickal traditions surrounding the ancient Nordic alphabet commonly known as the runes. Not only does this book delve into the correspondences associated with each letter of the Elder Futhark runes, it also gives instructions on magickal practices associated with the runes.

Other divination methods

Cary F. Baynes, translator
The Richard Wilhelm Translation of the I Ching, or Book of Changes

This is the granddaddy of I Ching books, featuring a fore-word by Carl Jung. Instead of a watered-down interpretation of the I Ching, this is an actual translation of the classic text, allowing the English-speaking reader the closest possible access to the ancient Chinese masterpiece.

Ellin Dodge
Numerology Has Your Number

An introduction to the science and art of numerology, pro-viding the key correspondences, challenges, and opportunities for each of the nine numbers. Includes exercises for determin-ing your personal numbers based on your name and date of birth, with practical information on the implications your numbers have for your life journey.

Judith Hipskind
Palmistry: the Whole View

Judith Hipskind
The New Palmistry: How to Read the Whole Hand and Knuckles

Like dream interpretation, palm reading offers access to the wisdom directly encoded in our bodies. Hipskind's books provide clear and useful instruction in the art. *The New Palmistry* supplements traditional palm reading with knuckle reading, providing even more information on the secrets hid-den in the hands.

Margaret Lange McWhorter
Tea Cup Tales: The Art of Tea Leaf Reading

Reading tea leaves hearkens back to the days of Victorian spiritualism, and it lives on today in New Orleans. In this delightful gift book, McWhorter provides the history and lore associated with tea leaf reading, along with numerous illustrated examples.

RITUAL

A ritual unites the energies of meditation and magick in a choreography of the spirit.

Like meditation, an effective ritual opens the heart and mind to focus on spiritual energies. It seeks union with the Goddess and the God through openness and receptivity. Like magick, a ritual changes things—at the very least it changes the participants, and the best rituals facilitate its participants' healing work in the world. And like a beautifully choreographed dance, effective rituals involve movement, action, and drama.

Ritual may be defined as an action or actions designed to foster communication with the Spirit realm. A ritual act can be as simple as lighting a candle to foster a contemplative ambience before meditating, or as complex as an intricate circle casting and drawing down ceremony performed at Samhain.

Witches typically love to participate in, and lead, ritual. On the night of the full or new moons, as well as on ancient Celtic holidays like Imbolc or Beltane, Wiccan solitaries and covens create sacred space and time through the act of casting a circle. In this circle (a world between the worlds), the Witches invoke the God and Goddess; raise magickal energies for healing or other benevolent purposes; and share the blessings of the Divine, usually through a ceremonial meal of food and drink, such as cakes and ale. The feel of most Wiccan rituals tends to blend an almost childlike sense of wonder and reverence with an upbeat, sometimes even playful, spirit. The emphasis is on mirth and pleasure, not repentance and self-criticism. Wiccan ceremonies are not designed to please an angry God, but rather seek to re-link the participants to the natural rhythms and processes of Mother Earth. At Beltane (May 1), Witches conjure forth the life-giving energies of Summer, while six months later as the "lifelessness" of Winter approaches, they remember their ancestors and those who have died. Whether large circles attended by hundreds of Pagans, or private rituals a solitary Wiccan performs in her or his home, these ceremonies foster healing, happiness, and wholeness—calling upon the love of the Gods to fill our lives and the lives of those we love with abundance and well-being.

A well-read Witch needs to know the theory and practice of writing and leading rituals, for Wicca is one of the few religions that actively encourages its participants to develop their own ritual skills and style. Some religions operate under the notion that ritual is something the clergy do while the laypeople simply watch or sing along during the hymns. Not so in the Craft. While covens or groves naturally have their best ritualists lead large ceremonies, every Witch learns enough about ritual to perform their own private ceremonies and to assist and eventually lead groups rituals (if they choose). Ritual leadership, like all spiritual power, is something Witches believe belongs to everyone, not just to a ministerial elite.

Renee Beck and Sydney Barbara Metrick,
The Art of Ritual: A Guide to Creating and Performing Your Own Ceremonies for Growth and Change

From the cover design showing a ceremony for drawing down the moon, to helpful and concise explanations of energy work and the role of the four Elements in ritual, to sections on such topics as consecrating tools and setting up an altar, this book exudes Wiccan sensibility. The authors examine the various building blocks of a successful ritual and provide step-by-step instructions for creating and enacting rituals large and small.

Blacksun
The Spell of Making

Detailed, step-by-step instructions of the ritual process, with an emphasis on the magickal dimension of each step in the ritual. A valuable book which includes considerations of the relationship between ritual and the unconscious, the relationship between ritual and mundane life, and the esoteric mystery dimension of Wiccan ritual.

Ivo Domínguez, Jr. - Panpipe
Castings: The Creation of Sacred Space

A study of the magick involved in the ritual movement toward higher realms, a process known variously as casting the circle or creating sacred space. Lots of esoteric information in here, including, but also going beyond, the normal Elemental/directional process to explore such lesser-known rituals as the Triangle of Stillness and the Square of Abeyance.

Peg Streep
Altars Made Easy: A Complete Guide to Creating Your Own Sacred Space

Setting up an altar—a focal point for your ritual and magickal work—is an important part of any Witch's spiritual practice. Creating an altar is like planting a garden: it can be formal and structured, or more wild in its layout. Some traditional Craft lineages have precise instructions on how to lay out an altar, while less formal groups and traditions allow for almost unlimited creativity. Either way, this book can deepen your understanding of sacred space and the role that designing, building, and using an altar can play in your spiritual life.

Margie McArthur
Wisdom of the Elements: The Sacred Wheel of Earth, Air, Fire, and Water

Nearly all Wiccan and eclectic Pagan traditions organize rituals around honoring the four directions (East, South, West, North) and the Elements associated with each direction. This book brims with Elemental lore, correspondences, and practices. While ritual is not the main focus, the information presented here will help anyone involved in Wiccan ritual to more fully understand the majesty of the Elements and their role in sacred ceremonies.

Nigel Pennick
Crossing the Borderlines: Guising, Masking & Ritual Animal Disguises in the European Tradition

This book looks at how the ceremonial dimension of folk practices can help modern Pagans create new rituals. From Morris Dancers to May Day revels, folk customs have an earthy dimension that hearken back to the rituals of old (see Chapter 22 for more information on the relationship between folklore and Paganism). Folk customs are a reminder that ritual involves the entire body through dance, performance, and the use of masks and costumes—a good ritual involves more than just a head trip.

Marion Weinstein
Earth Magic, A Dianic Book of Shadows: A Guide for Witches, Fourth edition

As an outgrowth of the author's personal book of shadows, *Earth Magic* includes basic instruction on the practice of magick, along with plenty of information on creating your own rites. Weinstein's vision of Wicca is deeply ethical, strongly feminist, and egalitarian. She brings those sensibilities to this book, and its strength lies in its values-based approach. Incidentally, for Weinstein, Dianic Wicca is feminist, but not exclusionary to men (or to the God).

Ed Fitch
Magical Rites from the Crystal Well

This book collects a number of rituals and essays on Pagan lore originally published in a periodical called, not surprisingly, *The Crystal Well*. Filled with beautiful pen and ink illustrations by John Goodier, it functions as an excellent resource for both beginners and experienced Wiccans, including seasonal rites, magickal workings, earth magick, and rites of passage.

Caitlín Matthews
Celtic Devotional: Daily Prayers and Blessings

A beautifully illustrated collection of Celtic rituals for personal use, with morning and evening invocations, meditations, and poems for throughout the year. The devotions flow with the lilting cadence of Celtic blessings (such as can be found in Carmichael's *Carmina Gadelica*, profiled in Chapter 22).

Starhawk, M. Macha Nightmare & the Reclaiming Collective
The Pagan Book of Living and Dying: Practical Rituals, Prayers, Blessings, and Meditations on Crossing Over

Rituals and background information on Pagan approaches to death and the dying process. For anyone who is concerned with death, is facing or has faced the death of a loved one, or provides spiritual support to the bereaved, this is an invaluable resource.

Paul V. Beyerl
A Wiccan Bardo, Revisited: Initiation and Self-Transformation

A collection of rituals from Beyerl's Tradition of Lothloriën, including basic rituals, pathworking, initiatory rites, and rites of passage. As a bonus, this book contains a collection of brief essays by the author on a variety of topics, ranging from the education of Pagan children to the necessity of ensuring your relatives will honor your wish for a Pagan funeral.

Pauline and Dan Campanelli
Pagan Rites of Passage

Rituals for the entire lifespan, beginning with the Wiccaning of a newborn, coming of age rituals, initiation, handfasting, midlife, the ordination of priests and priestesses, elderhood/croning, and rites for the dead. More than just a collection of rituals, each section includes background information on the significance of the passage, as well as traditional lore associated with that transition.

Herman Slater
A Book of Pagan Rituals

A classic of Craft literature, first published in the mid-1970s. Slater was the proprietor of the Magickal Childe, a legendary occult shop and publisher in New York City. Included in this collection are rituals of dedication, invocation, evocation, rites of passage, and rites of healing and purification.

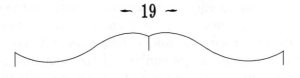

19

HEALING

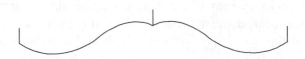

Witches heal.

Healing plays a fundamental role in the old religion. One of the primary traditions out of which modern Wicca developed is that of the village healers, the wise women and men who functioned as midwives, herbalists, and counselors, the ones who knew how to apply the properties of the natural world to strengthen the bodies and minds of all members of their communities. And so today, Wiccans practice magick, divination, ritual, and psychic skill as means to the end of healing, not just for themselves, but for all who come to them for help.

The coming of the modern era meant not only the consolidation of spiritual power into the bureaucracy of wealthy and powerful churches; it also meant the consolidation of healing arts into an increasingly arrogant medical profession. Without meaning to discount the many ways in which medical doctors have contributed to longevity and increasing quality of life, the rise of modern medicine has not come without a price. Mainstream medicine tends to treat the human body almost like a machine, on which the trained physician operates much like a mechanic repairs a car. While such objectivism in healthcare may have its place in some circumstances, it has also resulted in a runaway pharmaceutical culture, billions of dollars of unnecessary surgery, and the often unintended consequence of quality of life diminished as patients languish in sterile hospital environments, kept alive by the miracles of technology, but with little or no true beauty in their experience.

As natural healers, Witches do not replace, but complement, the work of physicians. Where doctors can perform a bypass to treat heart disease, reiki and other psychic forms of treatment can bring love and a sense of belonging to a lonely heart. Chemotherapy and radiation may be able to arrest or reverse cancerous growth, but ritual, healthy eating, and loving relationships can foster wellness in body and soul that is just as essential to true wellness. It is no accident that the revival of Witchcraft parallels the explosion of interest in alternative forms of healing. Of course, not all alternative healthcare providers are Wiccan, but all do stand in a long and proud tradition of holistic care that has been the province of the herbalist, folk-healer, and Witch, since time immemorial.

Janet and Stewart Farrar and Gavin Bone
The Healing Craft: Healing Practices for Witches and Pagans

A useful overview of magickal and alternative healing practices. The authors have a holistic approach to their subject, considering healing in physical, mental, spiritual, and magickal terms. Covering herbalism, healing properties of wells and springs, and the role of ritual, magick, divination, and shamanism in healing, this is probably the one book to read first when you begin to explore the relationship between the old religion and the healing arts.

Andrew Weil
Natural Health, Natural Medicine: A Comprehensive Manual for Wellness and Self-Care

Dr. Weil brought a level of legitimacy to the alternative health world—here was a Harvard-trained physician, advocating herbal supplements, meditation, and other alternative practices as a core element of healthcare. First published in the late 1980s and now completely revised and updated, this book provides a solid introduction to the sensible ways in which mainstream medicine and alternative healing practices can work together.

Diane Stein
All Women Are Healers: A Comprehensive Guide to Natural Healing

In the decade since this book first appeared, natural healing has become much more accepted within mainstream culture; now hospitals have meditation rooms and nurses practice reiki. So it's easy to forget that, not so long ago, such natural or alternative therapies were dismissed by the medical establishment and were only seriously embraced by a small segment of the population (including, of course, the Wiccan community). In this book, Diane Stein provides a useful overview of the varieties of natural healing practices, clearly linking alternative health to the wise woman tradition which is one of the foundations of modern Witchcraft.

Jeanne Achterberg, Ph.D., Barbara Dossey, R.N., M.S., FAAN, and Leslie Kolkmeier, R.N., M.Ed.
Rituals of Healing: Using Imagery for Health and Wellness

The authors—a psychologist and two nurses—celebrate the mind/body connection and its role in healing, by showing the relationship between visualization, imagination, and physical wellness. But this is more than just a book about affirmations;

the authors advocate creating and using rituals as an important part of the healing journey (this is not news to Witches, but it's fun to find a mainstream book endorsing what Goddess spirituality has taught all along).

Nina L. Diamond
Purify Your Body: Natural Remedies for Detoxing from Fifty Everyday Situations

Our body's natural wellness often suffers because of toxic elements in our lifestyle. Poor diet, lack of exercise, stressful driving or work situations, not drinking enough water, too much alcohol or caffeine—these are among the stressors we place on our bodies on a daily basis. Fortunately, there's a lot we can do to reduce the stress, and release or eliminate toxins from our bodies. Nina Diamond considers a variety of holistic treatments designed to strengthen and purify the body's natural ability for self-healing, including herbal and nutritional supplements, ayurveda, acupressure, and massage.

Julia Lorusso and Joel Glick
Healing Stoned: The Therapeutic Use of Gems and Minerals

A slender volume of crystal lore, published well before crystals become synonymous in the public eye with the New Age movement. With information on over 80 gemstones, this is a simple and straightforward classic that your coven elders probably used when they were first learning about crystal healing.

Gay Hendricks, Ph.D.
Conscious Breathing: Breathwork for Health, Stress Release, and Personal Mastery

Learning to breathe properly and effectively is one of the simplest ways to improve health, energy, and vitality. This book provides insight into the holistic benefits of full, deep, relaxed breathing, along with exercises to help the reader improve his or her breathwork. The book also includes information on breathing as a tool to enhance sports performance as well as sexual activity.

George Downing and Anne Kent Rush (illustrator)
The Massage Book

An elegantly simple textbook on the basics of full body massage, designed for the ordinary person who wishes to rub a friend to bliss. The author points out how the state of consciousness one achieves after a good massage is similar to the state attained through daily meditation. The implication for Wiccans: Massage can make for a delightful spiritual practice. And of course, it's a healing practice as well.

Anodea Judith
Wheels of Life: A User's Guide to the Chakra System

A comprehensive overview of the spinning wheels of light located throughout the human body. Most spiritual or psychic healing practices involve care for the chakra system; this book gives a basic grounding in understanding the different qualities of the seven main chakras, with material on the role the chakras play in magick, healing, divination, meditation, and manifestation.

Diane Stein
Essential Reiki: A Complete Guide to an Ancient Healing Art

Reiki (universal life-force energy) has become one of the most popular of healing touch practices. Like Wicca, reiki practice requires both knowledge and experience. To practice reiki, one must receive one or more attunements from a reiki master; as far as learning the history, theory and techniques of reiki, this book covers all the basics.

Barbara Ann Brennan
Hands of Light: A Guide to Healing Through the Human Energy Field

Another approach to the use of hands as instruments of spiritual/psychic healing, exploring the nature of the human aura and the techniques of healing energy work. Wonderful illustrations provide a graphic depiction of the chakras, the aura, and the benefits of healing touch.

The Boston Women's Health Book Collective
Our Bodies, Ourselves for the New Century: A Book by and For Women

A classic text not only of alternative health, but of feminism, this book led the way for women who sought to reclaim their healthcare from the institutionalized patriarchal medical establishment. With information relevant to women of diverse ethnic backgrounds and sexual orientations, this book is not only a must for all women concerned about their own health, but also belongs in the library of every Witch (yes, even guy Witches) who may be in a position of supporting women in their healing journey.

Jack Croft, editor
The Doctors' Book of Home Remedies for Men, From Heart Disease and Headaches to Flabby Abs and Fatigue

A big book of common-sense information about health issues specifically for men. Causes and remedies for over 150 health problems, along with an "In case of emergency" section covering serious situations like choking and frostbite. Although not as ideologically oriented toward alternative health as some of the other books profiled here, this is still a useful reference for Wiccans because of its advocacy of self-care.

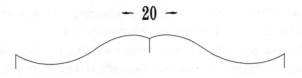

20

HERBALISM

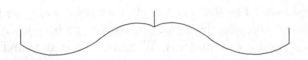

In *A Witches' Bible*, Janet and Stewart Farrar suggest that Wiccan healing practices fall under four main categories: spellcraft, psychological healing, energy work, and herbal remedies. We considered spellcraft in Chapter 16, energy work in the last chapter, and we'll look at psychology's role within the Craft in Chapter 29. Now we turn our attention to the significant role herbs play within the old religion.

Since ancient times, humankind has relied on the medicinal value of plants. Before there were drugs, there were herbs; and many plants have profound abilities to heal, alter mood, aid digestion, reduce fever, and otherwise support our physical and/or mental well-being. Indeed, up until recent times, even most drugs originated in the world of plant medicine; for example, aspirin is derived from the bark of the willow tree. Some herbs have become so well known for their healing properties that they can be found in the corner grocery or drug store: St. John's wort for the alleviation of depression; echinacea to boost immunity and fight colds, and ginseng to perk up the sex drive. Yet these popular herbs represent only the tiniest first steps into the vast storehouse of botanical remedies.

Witches not only use botanical products for healing, but for occult purposes as well. Herbs often figure prominently in the creation of magick potions and brews, and many spells call for one or more herbs as a significant ingredient. Plants with magickal associations also contribute to the incense and oils that Wiccans use in ritual and spells.

In addition to their magickal and healing properties, many herbs may be used simply as culinary delights. Where would the pleasures of the dinner table be without oregano, cumin, dill, and mint? For that matter, even simply growing an herb garden and enjoying the sights and smells can be a joyful un-dertaking and a sensual treat. Wiccans, who understand that herbs represent one way for re-connecting with the wisdom and beauty of Nature, find value in each of these aspects of herbs: medicinal, magickal, culinary, and horticultural. Chapter 32 (Kitchen Witchery) contains more books with herbal informa-tion, especially in terms of the kitchen or the garden.

A few important notes: a Witch cannot prescribe herbs like they were drugs (unless he or she is a physician), nor should herbal remedies be seen as sufficient to replace traditional medicine altogether. The role of Wicca as a healing spiritual practice means that it complements, not contradicts, the proper use of mainstream medicine. Also, when it comes to eating herbs (or drinking teas and tinctures), always consult a reputable teacher or reference book: some plants used for magickal work or grown for their beauty may not be safe for human consump-tion. If you wish to study herbs for their medicinal value, look for a qualified herbal master to teach you. The books profiled here can serve as reference works and textbooks for your stud-ies, but if you aspire to become a master herbalist, your first task is to find a mentor.

Susun S. Weed
Wise Woman Herbal for the Childbearing Year

Susun S. Weed
Wise Woman Herbal: Healing Wise

Two classic herbal texts by a well-respected greenwitch, herbalist, and keeper of the wise woman tradition. As the titles suggest, *Childbearing Year* covers herbs for use before, during, and after pregnancy; while *Healing Wise* provides general information on the healing properties of plants. By comparing the wise woman tradition to other elements of our culture, the author gives insight into just how revolutionary it is to reclaim the herbal healing practices. Both books feature attractive pen and ink illustrations.

Paul Beyerl
The Master Book of Herbalism

Paul Beyerl
A Compendium of Herbal Magick

In addition to being a master herbalist, Beyerl is a High Priest of the Craft. His first herbal book, *The Master Book*, incorporates information on both the remedial (medicinal) and magickal use of plants. The *Compendium* focuses almost entirely on magickal use, with an even larger listing of herbs than *The Master Book*. Beyerl's writing is straightforward and charming; his knowledge of lore appears encyclopedic. Great resources for those who want to delve into the mystical associations of herbs.

Richard Mabey et. al.
The New Age Herbalist

Many herbal books are beautifully designed, and this is no exception. Filled with gorgeous color illustrations and a glossary of 200 herbs, this book provides information on not only the culinary and medicinal use of botanicals, but also how herbs may be used for beauty and skin care, housekeeping, and decoration.

James A. Duke, Ph.D.
The Green Pharmacy: New Discoveries in Herbal Remedies for Common Diseases and Conditions from the World's Foremost Authority on Healing Herbs

Written for the general public and not specifically for Wiccans, this book describes herbal healing powers without resorting to magickal language—the tone is straightforward and scientific. Just as a gourmet chef is the best person to teach you about the culinary use of herbs, so a well-respected scientist like Duke is a fine guide to the healing plants. Arranged not by herb, but by disease or condition, this book provides a quick overview of every plant that may be beneficial (or, for that matter, harmful) to a given problem. The book contains nuggets of information on teas to brew, foods to eat, and overall lifestyle habits to promote health.

Jethro Kloss
Back to Eden, Revised and updated edition

Truly the granddaddy of modern herbal books, Kloss's 900-page book has served as a definitive guide to herbal medicine and therapy, natural foods, and home remedies for over 60 years now. The perfect title for anyone who thinks herbalism is just a New Age fad, this book combines a folksy style with lots of information on various medicinal plants, along with cross-references showing which herbs to use in treating various ailments. The book was revised by the Kloss family in the early 1970s. The language in it is staunchly Christian, but the information is universal.

Deni Bown
The Herb Society of America Encyclopedia of Herbs and Their Uses

Combining definitive information with gorgeous illustrations, this reference work includes entries on over a thousand different plants from around the world. Combining a catalog of in-depth information with a dictionary listing providing essential data, and detailing the culinary and medicinal uses of each plant, this is a book as useful as it is beautiful.

Ellen Evert Hopman
A Druid's Herbal for the Sacred Earth Year

Known both as a leader of the Pagan Druid community and as a master herbalist, Hopman combines her skills in this guide to herbs for each of the eight Pagan festivals. Since the Druid's year celebrates the same holidays as the Wiccan year, this is a book any Witch could use to learn about herbal correspondences for the Sabbats.

Jack Sanders
Hedgemaids and Fairy Candles: The Lives and Lore of North American Wildflowers

A celebration of more than 80 North American plants, packed full of medicinal, literary, and botanical information. Not really an herbal guide nor designed to identify wild plants, this book simply gets into the history and folklore of the plants it covers. Use jewelweed to relieve the itching caused by poison ivy, but fleabane, alas, does not live up to its name. Read this one not for easy access to practical information, but for the slow joy of discovery as the author takes you on a leisurely tour through America's untamed flora.

Judith Berger
Herbal Rituals

A month-by-month journey through the rhythms of the seasons, focussing on just one or two plants for each month. Rather than being a comprehensive guide to herbs, this book gets up close and personal with a handful of plants (such as mugwort, lavender, and rosemary), considering a variety of ways each plant can be used: as food or tea, in rituals or remedies. Taken as a whole, it's a yearlong journey toward getting to know a select few herbs—and cultivating a way of relating to the natural world based on appreciation, reverence, and spiritual observance.

Patricia Kaminski and Richard Katz
Flower Essence Repertory

A huge reference work on the many uses of flower essences for emotional, spiritual, and physical well-being. The use of flower essences for healing began with Dr. Edward Bach in England in the early 20th century; this book not only expands on Bach's work, but also includes many North American flowers not used by Bach.

Gaea and Shandor Weiss
Growing and Using Healing Herbs

An encyclopedia of plants to be grown in the garden and then used for their healing properties. Over 60 plants are included, with information on cultivating, harvesting, and preparing the parts of the plant used medicinally.

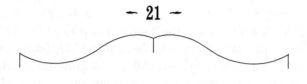

21

Cycles of the Sun and Moon

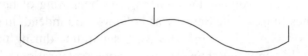

The human concept of time arises out of our experience of Natural cycles. The earth spins on its axis; forming the cycle of day and night. The moon, in relation to the sun and the night sky, appears to wax full, and then wane to darkness; each cycle lasting approximately one month. The earth revolves around the sun, and in doing so goes through four seasons; each of these cycles lasts a year. Other units of time, from milliseconds to millennia, are all merely divisions or multiples of these basic units of day, month, and year—each of which is based in the interplay between sun, moon, and earth.

Wiccan spirituality honors the cycles of the sun and the moon. These two cycles provide the foundation for the two forms of Wiccan ritual, the Sabbats and the Esbats.

Sabbats include eight major holidays, four of which are astronomical in origin and the other four of which date back to ancient Celtic agricultural practices. The astronomical (or lesser) Sabbats include Yule (the Winter Solstice), Ostara (the Spring Equinox), Litha (the Summer Solstice), and Mabon (the Fall Equinox). The greater Sabbats include Samhain (October 31)—a festival of death and new beginnings, celebrated at the end of harvest when in ancient times animals were slaughtered for the Winter's food supply; Imbolc (February 2)—a festival celebrating the coming of Spring, originally timed to coincide with the lactation of pregnant ewes; Beltane (May 1)—heralding the arrival of Summer, with powerful fertility rituals and joyful celebrations, some of which (like the Maypole dance) have survived as popular folk customs; and Lughnasadh (August 1)—marking the beginning of harvest. Witches think of the Sabbats as holidays, and indeed, in some traditions several covens who work separately during the lunar cycle come together for large Sabbat celebrations.

Esbats (which many Wiccans prefer to simply call "moons") occur strictly in accordance with the monthly cycle of new and full moons. Some Witches honor only the full moon, while others honor both full and dark moons. Witchcraft has long been associated with the magickal power of the moon, a magickal power which replicates itself in the deep intuitive wisdom and life-giving potential of the menstrual cycle.

The cycle of the Sabbats is the grand narrative of Demeter and Persephone, of the Goddess spending half the year blessing the land with fertility and abundance, and half the year mourning the loss of her daughter to the dread Lord of the Underworld, a time of scarcity and desolation. Many Witches divide the year into the Goddess's half and the God's half, with ritual observances to mark the transitions. The lunar cycle is seen not in such global terms; rather, the moons are times for working magick, developing intuition and psychic ability, and healing.

The books profiled in this chapter pertain to the spirituality of the sun or the moon, or to the ritual cycles associated with these heavenly bodies. In various ways, each of these books provides information that Wiccans can use in understanding and developing rituals to mark the passage of time and to celebrate the sweeping rhythms of Nature.

Ronald Hutton
The Stations of the Sun: A History of the Ritual Year in Britain

Hutton, author of the magisterial history of Wicca *The Triumph of the Moon*, here embarks on a similarly scholarly tour through the rituals and ceremonies marking the passage of time, as preserved in British myth, folklore, and custom. Christian, Pagan, and secular practices all come under scrutiny, and Hutton fearlessly debunks misunderstandings that have grown up around different practices.

Anne Kent Rush
Moon, Moon

A homegrown, hippie/feminist classic from the mid-1970s and the best single volume on moonlore that I have ever seen. When I first began to explore Paganism, this book was still in print, and like a fool I didn't buy a copy. Years later, I found an expensive, used copy via the Internet; when I showed it to a friend, she commented on its having been required reading when she was a Wiccan neophyte. It's certainly worth tracking down, for it contains in one oversized volume a treasury of moon myth, legend, ritual, and lore, perfect for anyone who wants to add a little lunacy to their spiritual practice.

Pauline and Dan Campanelli
Wheel of the Year: Living the Magical Life

A charming tour through the calendar holidays, with rituals, exercises, and recipes for each month of the year. Much of the material presented here is family friendly, enabling both adults and children in a Wiccan household to share their spiritual practice.

Edain McCoy
The Sabbats: A New Approach to Living the Old Ways

For each of the eight holidays; McCoy provides background information on the lore surrounding the day, along with sample recipes and craft ideas appropriate for the season. Ritual ideas for both solitaries and groups are provided, along with charts of correspondences for those who wish to write their own rituals.

Máire MacNeill
The Festival of Lughnasa: A Study of the Survival of the Celtic Festival of the Beginning of Harvest

First published in 1962, this 700-page scholarly monograph concerns just one element of the Pagan past—the festival of Lughnasa (Lammas), the first harvest festival celebrated in late July/early August. MacNeill documents festivals, assemblies, fairs, myths, and legends all associated with this single holiday. More than just a compendium of folklore, this precious glimpse into vanishing old ways provides valuable insight into the thematic and ritual elements of Paganism that were strong enough to survive into modern times.

Silver RavenWolf
Halloween: Customs, Recipes & Spells

An anthology of facts, lore, ritual ideas, and other suggestions on how to make the most out of the witchiest night of the year. Chapters on "Halloween in the Kitchen" and "A Time to Honor the Dead" provide details on the many ways in which to celebrate this Sabbat.

Nigel Pennick
The Pagan Book of Days: A Guide to the Festivals,
Traditions, and Sacred Days of the Year

If you'd like to take your sense of Pagan spiritual rhythms a
level deeper than simply honoring the Sabbats and moons, the
information in this book can guide you. Following the standard
calendar (January-December), this book documents traditional
and Pagan lore associated with each of the months, and with
specific days throughout the year.

Alexei Kondratiev
The Apple Branch: A Path to Celtic Ritual

Although this intelligent and thoughtful book primarily dis-
cusses ritual, it is not really a book about Wiccan ceremonies,
but rather a non-sectarian Celtic approach to ritual that would
be appropriate for Wiccans, Druids, other forms of Pagans, or
even Christians. Yet even Witches with no interest in such interfaith work will still find Kondratiev's detailed discussions of
the history and lore associated with the Wheel of the Year well
worth checking out.

Janice Broch and Veronica MacLer
Seasonal Dance: How to Celebrate the Pagan Year

Another trip around the Wheel of the Year, with sample
rituals for each of the Sabbats. For those who like to have movement in your spiritual practice, check out the appendix with
information on various circle dances.

Lori Reid
Moon Magic: How to Use the Moon's Phases to Inspire and
Influence Your Relationships, Home Life and Business

A brief introduction to the astrology of the moon, considering the energies involved with the moon's position in each
of the 12 signs; factors well worth considering when planning

magickal working and rituals (especially full moon rituals). Here's a tip: at each full moon, the moon is in the opposite sign from the sun. So when the sun is in Aries, the full moon that month is in Libra; when the sun is in Taurus, the full moon that month is in Scorpio, and so on. Using this book can help plan full moon rituals that work with, rather than against, the energy of the moon's placement in the sky.

Ute York
Living By the Moon: A Practical Guide to Choosing the Right Time

A straightforward approach to gardening, health and beauty issues, family and professional concerns, and of course magickal and spiritual matters, all based on the phases of the moon as well as the moon's astrological transits. Reading through this book and applying its advice can help to cultivate an overall sense of magick in life, as each week brings a new moon phase with its practical correspondences.

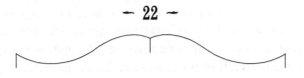

22

FOLKLORE

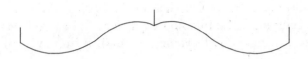

At the time of the Winter Solstice, hang a sprig of mistletoe in your house for couples to kiss beneath...Around the time of the Spring Equinox, hide eggs in the garden for children to find...On May 1, dance around the Maypole, ribbons swirling in the bright blue sky to celebrate the coming of Summer...On October 31, watch out for the children dressed as ghosts and goblins, traversing the streets seeking treats from their "frightened" neighbors.

These practices, deeply entrenched within our culture, help us to understand and mark the passage of time. Such ancient folk customs have survived despite both political and religious changes over the centuries. Even though such customs are Pagan in origin, Christians love to kiss under their Christmas mistletoe and hunt for their Easter eggs. Not that there's anything wrong with Christians or anyone else enjoying Pagan folk practices (most Witches would heartily encourage non-Wiccans to enjoy these meaningful and enjoyable customs); they're simply solid evidence of how the old ways have survived, even centuries after new religious ideas became dominant in Europe.

In reviving pre-Christian forms of European spirituality, Wicca draws much of its inspiration from the surviving folklore and folk customs throughout Europe (and America). Although such traditions often seem to be fragmented and devoid of meaning, research into Pagan mythology reveals how much of folklore actually honors the old ways. For example: A bunny that hides eggs may seem like nothing more than a quaint practice for Easter celebrations; but these customs make plenty of sense when we see how Easter takes its name from Ostara, a Norse Goddess of the Spring, the dawn, and new beginnings. Rabbits and eggs were her sacred symbols. So this charming child's game is actually a ritual way of honoring the Goddess.

The books mentioned in this chapter celebrate the vast storehouse of folklore, focusing primarily on English and Celtic traditions. In today's media-frenzied, television/Internet soaked world, when folk tales, songs, and customs are rapidly disappearing, such material is priceless. Wiccans need to know folklore, for these treasures provide not only insights into ways to revive ancient practices, but also insights into the values, practices, and beliefs of people who live close to the earth. If nothing else, folklore reminds us that modern Wicca is far more than the fantasy of a few 20th-century Occultists; it's a meaningful revival of an ancient and powerful spiritual wellspring.

Robert A. Georges and Michael Owen Jones
Folkloristics: An Introduction

If your interest in folklore goes beyond merely trying to collect some neat stories, and you wish to bring scholarly rigor to your studies, this is a useful introduction. It's an undergraduate textbook detailing the study of folklore and folklore methodologies, along with considering the impact of folklore on other aspects of popular culture.

Janet and Colin Bord
Earth Rites: Fertility Practices in Pre-Industrial Britain

The Bords explore how the environmental degradation which characterizes our age derives, at least in part, from the loss of a spirituality grounded in the earth. This spirituality, the authors go on to show, was alive not very long ago and in some cases survives in folkloric ways to this very day. Exploring the magickal landscape of Great Britain through standing stones and holy wells, sacred trees and fertility customs, *Earth Rites* provides a compelling argument for the Pagan revival by showing that what is being revived has not been slumbering very long.

Maria Leach, editor
Funk & Wagnall's Standard Dictionary of Folklore, Mythology and Legend

This massive reference book contains more than 1,200 pages of mythic and folkloric data, making it a definitive sourcebook for both the academic specialist as well as the general reader interested in this topic. With more than 8,000 entries spanning cultures from around the globe, this is probably the best single-volume reference as yet available.

Walter L. Brenneman, Jr. and Mary G. Brenneman
Crossing the Circle at the Holy Wells of Ireland

Sacred wells played a significant role in the Pagan worldview of the ancient Druids; this book—part history, part travelogue, part study of popular folklore and piety—shows how that ancient reverence has survived, even if in a degenerate form, up to the present day. Photographs of many of the holy wells still to be found in Ireland illustrate this consideration of how the wells have functioned as sacred sites.

Brian Day
Chronicle of Celtic Folk Customs: A Day-to-Day Guide to Folk Traditions

Over 450 customs gathered from the six Celtic lands of Scotland, Ireland, Wales, Brittany, Cornwall, and the Isle of Man, arranged chronologically. Describing both existing and historical celebrations, rituals, dances, games, beliefs, and other practices, the book not only provides an overview of Celtic folk practices, but can help you find living folk practices as they happen in our time.

Jacqueline Simpson and Steve Roud
A Dictionary of English Folklore
Dáithí Ó hOgáin
Myth, Legend & Romance: An Encyclopedia of the Irish Folk Tradition

Respective reference works that delve deeply into the Celtic and Anglo-Saxon folk traditions (the two cultures that most directly influenced the development of modern Wicca). Scholarly in tone, these are books written by and for academics, but they are accessible for the general reader and highly useful to the average Witch. *Myth, Legend & Romance* has more explicitly Pagan material, because it includes in-depth consideration of the major figures in Irish mythology, both heroes (Fionn MacCumhaill) and deities (Brighid). Both books include plenty of Christianized folklore, much of which (for example, Brighid as a Christian saint in Ireland) often seems deeply rooted in Pagan tradition. Other topics covered include superstitions, legends, and historical figures whose lives carry mythical overtones.

F. Marian McNeill
The Silver Bough
(Volume One: Scottish Folklore and Folk-Belief; Volume Two: A Calendar of Scottish National Festivals: Candlemas to Harvest Home; Volume Three: A Calendar of Scottish National Festivals: Hallowe'en to Yule; Volume Four: The Local Festivals of Scotland)

Written close to half a century ago, these books contain errors understandable for their age, ranging from regarding Christianity as more "evolved" than Paganism, to accepting Margaret Murray's now-discredited theories about the nature of Witchcraft during the burning times. But for the discerning reader who overlooks those problems, a genuine treasure may be found here: over 650 pages of Scottish folklore and customs, ranging from key national observances to idiosyncratic local customs. The first book considers the role Druids and Witches played in the Scottish folk tradition; volumes two and three take an in-depth tour around the Wheel of the Year, while the final volume travels to a variety of settings to celebrate the many regional practices.

Robin Skelton and Margaret Blackwood
Earth, Air, Fire, Water: Pre-Christian and Pagan Elements in British Songs, Rhymes and Ballads

Witches and spells, magick and the Goddess, herbal lore and Fairy encounters—such themes appear repeatedly in the rich storehouse of British folk songs and rhymes. In this book, Skelton and Blackwood have collected some of the more obviously Pagan examples of the folk song/ballad tradition (see Chapter 33 for another collection of English ballads, more suitable for use in performance).

Julian Cope
The Modern Antiquarian: A Pre-Millennial Odyssey Through Megalithic Britain

Although primarily a gazetteer to some 300 pre-historic sites in the British isles, this book gathers folklore associated with such sites, along with the author's own story of visiting these sites over an eight-year period. Taken as a whole, it's a powerful testament to the pervasive presence of pre-Christian remains in Britain.

Alexander Carmichael
Carmina Gadelica: Hymns & Incantations Collected in the Highlands and Islands of Scotland in the Last Century

A splendid anthology of folk prayers, rhymes, invocations, blessings, curses, and various other pieces of the Scottish oral tradition, collected in Gaelic and translated by Carmichael, an amateur folklorist of the 19th century. Plenty of Christian imagery here, rubbing elbows with older, clearly Pagan material. Many members of the Wiccan community have re-Paganized some of the chants and prayers found here, for use in modern Craft rituals. This book will teach you more about authentic Celtic spirituality than all of the New Age-based Celtic books combined.

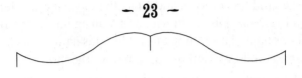

MYTHOLOGY

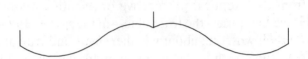

Wicca has no Bible or sacred scripture. Many Witches feel that Nature herself is the only, or truest, source of Divine revelation. To find the Goddess and the Green Man, better to consult a living tree than to spend time with a tree that has died and been converted to paper.

But just because there is no such thing as Wiccan scripture does not mean there is no place for ancient writings in the Craft. Wiccans often feel a deep love for the world's great mythological traditions. After all, we encounter the Gods and Goddesses in the realm of myth—that treasure house where the wisdom, lore, and exploits of the Gods have been passed down from generation to generation.

To understand the significance of mythology, look at how Greek and Roman myth continue to impact modern popular culture. Even after 2,000 years of monotheistic religion, the various Gods and Goddesses of southern Europe simply won't go away. It doesn't take a college education to know that Venus is the Goddess of love, and Mars the God of war. Hercules lives on in a Walt Disney movie, and Vulcan has a race of *Star Trek* aliens named after him. Saturn lent his name to a car company, and Apollo carried the first man to the moon.

But of course, the notion of "it's just a myth" persists in culture, suggesting that mythic stories of Gods and Goddesses are somehow not real. To Pagans, such attacks involve a sloppy use of empirical philosophy to evaluate spiritual material. Did a "real" Venus come to life from the foam of the sea? Did a "real" Odysseus take 20 years to travel home? Did a "real" Lancelot sleep with a "real" Guenivere? When we try to read myth from the skeptical perspective of scientific reason, we quickly lose the spirit—the true value—of the stories. But when we give up on worrying about whether myths are true and instead read them with a playful, open mind that allows higher truth to be revealed through stories that may or may not be based in history—that's when myth has the potential to teach, to inspire, to enlighten, to entertain, to transform us.

Well-read Witches can find wonder and insight in the magick of these stories that come from all over the world. The books profiled here include Native American, Egyptian, Celtic, and Chinese mythic traditions. Even if your lineage of Wicca works within only one mythological tradition (such as Egyptian or Celtic), much can be learned from the mythic wisdom of other cultures. Joseph Campbell's *The Hero With a Thousand Faces* and Jaan Puhvel's *Comparative Mythology* seek to understand myth by exploring themes and patterns that appear in different mythologies from different cultures.

None of this is holy writ—but all of it contains the potential of teaching universal truths under the guise of simple folktales.

Kevin Osborn and Dana L. Burgess, Ph.D.
The Complete Idiot's Guide to Classical Mythology

A basic survey of Greek and Roman myths, presented in an easy-to-use, reader-friendly format. From creation myths to heroic adventures, tales of Olympus and dark journeys into the underworld, this book retells the myths in a no-nonsense, straightforward way. Like other volumes in this series, its tone is lighthearted and accessible. A useful tool to make up for all that time you spent daydreaming back in high school.

Robert Graves
The White Goddess: A Historical Grammar of Poetic Myth

A visionary speculation on the nature the Great Goddess, depicting her as the ultimate source of all poetic and mythic language. Published in 1948, this book inspired the first generations of modern Wiccans and then lost credibility when critics like Isaac Bonewits and Ronald Hutton attacked the quality of its scholarship. If read as a literary tour de force rather than an academic treatise, it still deserves its place as a classic text of the Goddess renaissance.

Robert Graves
The Greek Myths

Literary retelling of the classical myths, from the author of *The White Goddess*. Tales of Gods and Goddesses, of this world and the underworld, of creation and battles (including the Trojan War), and of the exploits of heroes, including Heracles, Jason, and Odysseus.

Clive Barrett
The Egyptian Gods and Goddesses

Explore the riches of the Egyptian family of Gods and Goddesses in this readable anthology. Barrett not only tells the stories of over 30 Gods and Goddesses, but illustrates many of the deities in beautiful black and white graphics. Information about animals sacred to the Egyptians, the pyramids and mummification, and symbols used in Egyptian religion round out this handy introductory volume.

Charles Squire
Celtic Myth and Legend, Revised edition

First published nearly a century ago, this collection of stories from the Irish and Welsh traditions remains a favorite of Pagans and non-Pagans alike; it appears on the reading list of most Druid groups. It's a simple and easy-to-read retelling of the great stories; a classic in its own right. The revised edition includes a brief introduction by contemporary Wiccan author Sirona Knight.

Tom P. Cross and Clark Harris Slover, editors
Ancient Irish Tales

An anthology of Celtic myth remarkable not only for its size, but also for its comprehensive coverage. Key tales from each of the major Irish cycles are included: the mythological cycle (tales of Gods and Goddesses), the Ulster cycle (tales of Cuchulainn, the greatest of Irish heroes), the Fenian cycle (tales of Finn McCool, the Irish answer to King Arthur), and the so-called historical cycle, which includes tales of both legendary and historical Irish kings.

Alain Daniélou
The Myths and Gods of India: The Classic Work on Hindu Polytheism

This classic study of the Hindu tradition looks at the philosophy and cosmology of Indian religion, and examines key figures such as Kali, Vishnu, Shiva, Shakti, Brahma, along with other Vedic deities. With chapters devoted to mantras, yantras, worship, and ritual, this is an encyclopedic introduction to the Hindu path (which shares with European shamanism a common ancestry in Indo-European religion).

Sir James George Frazer
The Golden Bough: A Study in Magic and Religion

First published in 1922, this is one of the 20th century's greatest, if flawed, achievements in the area of primal spirituality. From Diana/Artemis through sympathetic magick, tree worship, incarnate gods, the sacred marriage, taboos and sacrifice, agricultural worship and fire festivals, topic after topic covered in this monumental work is of interest to Wiccans and others in the Nature spirituality community. Some of the scholarship in this book is considered questionable today, but overall it remains a majestic study of the most primal dimensions of the human quest for the spirit.

Hyemeyohsts Storm
Seven Arrows

A beautifully written and illustrated collection of Native American myths, stories, and teachings. At first challenging to the Western reader because it is written in a visionary, dreamlike, nonlinear way, to the seeker who approaches this book with an open mind, rich treasures await. Through vivid imagery and rich, detailed glimpses of the luminous beauty of Nature, the stories collected here weave a spell of enchantment grounded in the native ways of this land and its original people.

Clyde W. Ford
The Hero With An African Face: Mythic Wisdom of Traditional Africa

Thanks to the Golden Dawn and other magickal groups, the myths and Gods of Egypt are well known to most of today's Pagans. But for many Witches whose spirituality is often based almost entirely on Celtic or Mediterranean sources, the rich traditions of Africa outside of Egypt remain uncharted territory. This book can help Wiccans learn about both the deities and the philosophy of a variety of African cultures, from the Ashanti to the Yoruba.

Anne M. Birrell
Chinese Mythology: An Introduction

Tales of Gods and Goddesses, emperors and dynasties, and heroes and treachery form the fabric of this collection of some 300 Chinese tales, gathered from a variety of literary sources.

Jaan Puhvel
Comparative Mythology

A look at the similarities between different mythological traditions within the Indo-European family of cultures. Puhvel explores Celtic, Germanic, Baltic, Greco-Roman, Iranian, and Indian myths to identify central themes such as those involving the Warrior, the King, the Sacredness of Fire and Water, and similarities among the Gods. An excellent tool for Witches in that it shows the viability of "All Gods are one God, and all Goddesses are one Goddess." Trace different mythologies back far enough, and the unity among the deities begins to emerge.

Joseph Campbell
The Hero With a Thousand Faces

One of the most central themes in world mythology involves the hero's journey—the quest through trials and adventures in search of some sort of holy grail. This book, widely regarded as Campbell's masterpiece, considers examples from mythic traditions the world over to explore the "grammar of the symbols" and identify the core components of the hero's quest.

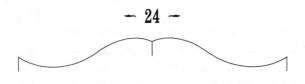

24

The Inspiration
of the Celts

The Celtic tradition has been one of the most important cultural sources for modern Witchcraft. Celtic deities like Cernunnos and Brighid are among the most loved Gods and Goddesses in Wiccan ritual, while the greater Sabbat holidays of Samhain, Imbolc, Beltane, and Lughnasadh are all Celtic in origin. It is through Celtic lore that Witches learn of the Fairy realms, the mysticism of trees, and the promise of a paradisiacal Summerland. If Wicca is not a purely Celtic spirituality (and actually, most Pagan Druids will insist it isn't), then at least it is an eclectic path with a decidedly Celtic flavor.

We don't know much about ancient Celtic religious practices. Scholars regard the most primal form of Celtic spirituality to be shamanistic in nature; although once the Celts developed a more complex culture, they also developed an official priesthood—who came to be known as the Druids. Druids were not only magicians and shamans, but also lawyers, philosophers, and counselors. Basically, the Druids were the keepers of wisdom. Alas, they did not write down their lore and secrets, sensibly recognizing that written material could easily fall into the wrong hands. Once the Romans conquered the Celtic lands and decimated the Druid order, the tradition was pushed underground, where it became the fragmented source of legends, superstition, and folklore. Thankfully, Irish and Welsh monks during the Dark Ages did attempt to preserve the ancient myths of their people, but often these written legends were altered to be acceptable within the new regime of Christianity; therefore, Gods were often demoted to saints, while Biblical imagery is often interwoven among the native Celtic tales. Fortunately, the Pagan renaissance of modern times has encouraged a new generation of Irish and Welsh scholars committed to retelling the ancient stories in ways that honor the old lore.

Celtic folklore and legend has continued to influence the spirituality of ordinary people well into modern times, primarily in terms of the Fairy faith—folk beliefs regarding the existence of Fairies and other Spirit Beings. Even among devout Celtic Christians, both in ancient and modern times, many Pagan beliefs and practices survived, a testament to the power of the Celtic soul.

Not every Wiccan lineage relies primarily on Celtic myth and culture. Different traditions focus on Egyptian, Italian, or Norse wisdom. Many Wiccan groups draw eclectic inspiration from a variety of different mythic and spiritual cultures. Such is the beautiful diversity of the Craft. If your tradition has a non-Celtic focus, Chapter 25 uncovers some of the treasures from cultures other than the Celts. In studying the cultures that inspire your tradition, you will appreciate more deeply the subtle symbols and hidden lessons found within your particular path. Making the effort to learn the ways of the ancestors (whether they are your actual blood ancestors or spiritual "ancestors of the soul") will only deepen and empower your experience as a Witch.

Caitlín and John Matthews
The Encyclopedia of Celtic Wisdom: A Celtic Shaman's Sourcebook

Earth spirituality, tree lore, ancestor and animal wisdom, initiation and shapeshifting, Druids and seers, prophets and diviners—the rich tapestry of Celtic myth, legend, and lore provides the backdrop on which this treasure trove of wisdom has been built. Drawing mainly from the Irish tradition, these stories, reflections, and rituals can assist anyone who wishes to cultivate a richly developed inner life in harmony with Celtic ways.

Dáithí Ó hÓgáin
The Sacred Isle: Belief and Religion in Pre-Christian Ireland

This scholarly introduction to Irish Paganism draws on archaeology, mythology, and folklore, although written in an accessible manner for readers who may not have an academic background. Beginning with the pre-Celtic Irish cultures, the book surveys Iron Age practices which led up to the flowering of Irish spirituality among the Druids. Concepts such as sovereignty, the sacredness of the land, and the nearness of the otherworld illuminate the rich heritage presented in this book.

R. J. Stewart
Celtic Gods, Celtic Goddesses

Learning about the Celtic family of Gods is no easy task. For one thing, Celtic religion never had a single pantheon— there was no one set of over-arching deities as found in Greek or Roman religion. Instead, various Celtic tribes and localities revered local deities, with only a few figures attaining a prominence that crossed tribal boundaries. R. J. Stewart has carefully balanced scholarship and spirituality in this overview of key figures including Brighid, Cernunnos, Mabon, the Morrigan, and Manannan.

Anne Ross
Pagan Celtic Britain: Studies in Iconography and Tradition

This monumental study considers archaeological sources to explore how Pagan religious and spiritual practices survived in the British Isles, even with the coming of the Roman and Christian conquests. Ross examines evidence for the veneration of Gods, Goddesses, sacred birds and other animals, and the veneration of sacred wells. Of particular interest to Wiccans is her study of reverence for horned Gods.

Alwyn Rees and Brinley Rees
Celtic Heritage: Ancient Tradition in Ireland and Wales

This book, deeply loved by the Pagan Druid community, explores the poetry and Fairy-landscape of Irish storytelling and myth. The authors explore the Irish concept of the sacred land and the five ancient provinces, considering how the sovereignty of the land informs the spirituality of Irish myth. From there they consider specific themes in the Irish storytelling tradition, including adventures, voyages, and youthful exploits. A luminous book that reads with the same kind of lilting mystery heard in the ancient tales themselves.

Caitlín Matthews
Mabon and the Mysteries of Britain: An Exploration of the Mabinogion

The *Mabinogion* includes the richest treasure trove of Welsh myth, and as such contains the deepest mysteries of the British Pagan tradition. The author explores the ancient text to plumb the mystery tradition and discover how its secrets still speak to us today. Weaving her interpretive narrative around the figures of Mabon (the shining youth) and Modron (his mother), Matthews reveals the interplay of Goddess and God in this branch of the Celtic tradition. When you read this, read *The Mabinogion* itself (available in several different editions) at the same time.

Philip Carr-Gomm
The Druid Way

A lovely meditation on the Druid revival in our time from the perspective of the author's adventure walking through the British countryside. In exploring the sacred landscape, Carr-Gomm finds plenty of inspiration for exploring the Celtic spirit. The text includes a wedding ceremony and funeral, thereby providing a sense of contemporary Druidic ritual.

W. Y. Evans-Wentz
The Fairy-Faith in Celtic Countries

First published in 1911, this book examines the tradition of Fairies in terms of documented examples of living people in the six Celtic lands who believed in, and/or encountered, Fairies. Several hundred pages of testimony that belief in Fairies survived heartily into the modern era.

Murry Hope
Practical Celtic Magic: A Working Guide to the Magical Heritage of the Celtic Races

More down-to-earth than many of the books profiled in this chapter, this handbook of magick written from a Celtic perspective looks at Irish, Welsh, and Arthurian traditions to explore how they contribute to modern Occultism. Tree magick, Druidic lore, Arthurian magick, and the Bardic tradition all contribute to this primer on Celtic esotericism.

John O'Donohue
Anam Cara: A Book of Celtic Wisdom

As beautifully written as an Irish love song, this poetic reflection on the spirituality of the modern Celts shows just how Pagan the Celtic people remain, even after 1,500 years of Christian occupation. O'Donohue, a Catholic priest, weaves mystical Christian and Pagan images and stories together in his celebration of the land, the imagination, and the essential earthiness of the body. Incidentally, the title comes from the Gaelic; it means "soul friend" and comes from a tradition that began with the Druids who served as counselors to the Celtic chieftains.

Miranda J. Green
Dictionary of Celtic Myth and Legend

James MacKillop
Dictionary of Celtic Mythology

Two handy reference books, both by respected Celtic scholars, both containing hundreds of entries drawn from Irish, Welsh, and continental sources.

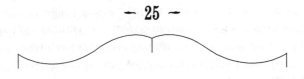

25

The Inspiration
of World Cultures

The last chapter explored the cultural and religious ways in which the Celtic races have inspired the modern expression of Wicca. If I had unlimited space and time to write this book, I'd love to include separate chapters on the Egyptians, the Greeks and Romans, the Native Americans, the Norse, and several other cultures.

But unlimited space and time are not currently at my disposal, so I have made a compromise: because my personal path draws inspiration primarily from the Celtic lands, I devoted an entire chapter to their culture, with this chapter providing a brief overview of cultural sources from around the world. I want to make clear that this distinction reflects my bias. Many Witches will want to explore the Egyptians or the Norse or (insert your favorite culture) with the same depth of research that I personally have put into studying the Celts.

This is as it should be. Wicca respects and honors all the positive paths of the world, without passing judgment or harsh criticism. You can safely assume that when a culture's religious, spiritual, or mythological tradition includes Goddess worship, magick, mysticism, shamanism, psychic development, or any other form of wisdom, Witches will be interested in it. In fact, the only cultural quality most Witches reject is intolerance. In 1974, The Council of American Witches issued a statement on the Principles of Wiccan Belief, which said in part: "Our only animosity toward...any other religion or philosophy-of-life, is to the extent that its institutions have claimed to be 'the only way' and have sought to deny freedom to others and to suppress other ways of religious practice and belief."

The books profiled in this chapter can help you to understand Witchcraft today by exploring ancient (and sometimes not-so-ancient) practices associated with primitive religion. Like Chapter 23's overview of mythology, the books included here cover a range of cultures, from Native America to India to Northern Europe. Rituals, initiation practices, explorations in consciousness, and other spiritual practices appear in the pages of these books. The only common denominator: each one celebrates one particular culture, which may or may not have bearing on any one tradition or lineage of Wicca. But even if your flavor of Wicca doesn't find much use in the Greek mysteries or the psychic somersaults performed by modern-day Yogis, remember that for other Pagans, these cultural sources deeply inspire their practice.

Many of these books contain bibliographies of their own, which can help you to explore that particular culture in greater depth. Rather than take my word for which cultures are the most important ones to study, rely on your own intuition or the traditions of your particular lineage. When in doubt, consult with your High Priestess or your spirit guides.

Walter Burkert
Greek Religion

Walter Burkert
Ancient Mystery Cults

Burkert is respected as one of the 20th century's foremost scholars of Greek religion. For those who do not have an affinity for academics, these books may seem imposing, but for anyone who wishes to have a thorough and in-depth knowledge of Greek paganism not solely as a collection of myths, but as a religious culture filled with ritual and meaning, these books are the essential place to begin. In *Greek Religion*, Burkert considers both archaeology and literary evidence to piece together the practice of Greek Paganism; *Ancient Mystery Cults* compares five Greek mysteries, taking pains to view ancient practices within a Pagan framework and sensibility.

Marvin W. Meyer, editor
The Ancient Mysteries: A Sourcebook of Sacred Texts

This can be used as a companion volume to the works of Walter Burkert, profiled above, although this anthology is larger in scope than just Greek religion—material from Syria, Egypt, Rome, and even Jewish and Christian sources are included here (Yes, Christianity is a mystery religion). What makes this text so important is that it includes translations of ancient texts themselves, allowing the practitioners, guardians, and observers of the ancient mysteries to speak with their own voice.

Apuleis (translated by Robert Graves)
The Transformations of Lucius Otherwise Known as The Golden Ass

Because Goddess spirituality has its roots in antiquity, it only stands to reason that many classic texts from the ancient world would appeal to Wiccan booklovers. It would be impossible for me to list all the ancient texts that contain material of interest to Witches. But this particular book deserves a mention for several reasons: not only because the translator is Goddess-booster Robert Graves (author of *The White Goddess*), but also because the story contains elements of shape-shifting and devotion to Isis, giving the reader a glimpse into the ways of the Goddess as ancient people themselves understood it.

Patrick Jasper Lee
We Borrow the Earth: An Intimate Portrait of the Gypsy Shamanic Tradition and Culture

Wiccan elders like Sibyl Leek and Raymond Buckland have acknowledged the deeply magickal tradition of the Gypsies (Romany) as a source of inspiration for modern Wicca. This book, written by a Romany, plumbs the author's experience as a Gypsy and explains key concepts of the misunderstood people's spirituality.

Paramahansa Yogananda
Autobiography of a Yogi

Yogananda was one of the earliest of Indian gurus to bring his message to the West and thus endeavored to present his message in a way that Westerners would find palatable. For example, he speaks of the Divine primarily as God. But he also acknowledges the feminine tradition of spirituality, making references to the Goddess Kali in the first chapter of the book. What makes this book especially useful is its colorful descriptions of mystical states of consciousness, such as samadhi (a state of Divine union).

David R. Kinsley
Hindu Goddesses: Visions of the Divine Feminine in the Hindu Religious Tradition

This academic study of the Goddess tradition in India considers both major and minor figures in the Hindu pantheon, tracing their history through sacred literature (the Vedas), religious practice, and identification of the Goddess with the land. Read this one in conjunction with Yogananda's more personal book to balance out his rather male-oriented views.

Elsa-Brita Titchenell
The Masks of Odin: Wisdom of the Ancient Norse

The Hindus called their sacred scripture the Vedas; in northern Europe the holy writings were called the Edda. If the two words seem similar, that's because they share a common Indo-European ancestry. Edda means grandmother, the matrix of the people's wisdom. This one volume introduction to Nordic Paganism that combines an introductory section on the indigenous spirituality of northern Europe with an anthology of elegantly translated Norse myths from the Poetic Edda.

Hilda Ellis Davidson
The Lost Beliefs of Northern Europe

Hilda Ellis Davidson
Myths and Symbols in Pagan Europe: Early Scandinavian and Celtic Religions

One of the most respected of Nordic scholars combines archaeology, religious studies, and folklore studies to consider the scope and nature of Norse Paganism. *Lost Beliefs* examines how the Gods appear in mythology and the cult practices associated with them, along with the spirituality of Goddesses, guardian spirits, and otherworld journeying. If some of this sounds as much Celtic as Nordic, then go on to read *Myths and Symbols in Pagan Europe*, in which Ellis Davidson explores the commonalities between Celtic and Nordic Paganism, as two branches of the Indo-European cultural tree.

John G. Neihardt
Black Elk Speaks: Being the Life Story of a Holy Man of the Oglala Sioux

Joseph Epes Brown
The Sacred Pipe: Black Elk's Account of the Seven Rites of the Oglala Sioux

The two books based on the life experience of Black Elk, a Lakota shaman, are classics in their genre. After almost half a century, they remain important glimpses into the rich culture of the Plains Indians. From sweatlodges to vision quests to the sun dance, the ways of the Native Americans are preserved here, as told through one of the most celebrated of Native shamans.

Charlotte Berney
Fundamentals of Hawaiian Mysticism

Showcasing the path of the Huna (the secret tradition of the Hawaiian people), Berney explores how the mysticism of Hawaii serves as a healing practice as well as a path of meditation and prayer. The author covers elements such as Hawaiian mythology, veneration of the ancestors, and the concept of mana (the life-force).

26

The Occult
Tradition

In Western culture, a grand tradition of magickal inquiry has inspired mystics and seekers for centuries. Drawing on esoteric sources such as the Kabbalah and the Tarot, and building on the work of famous magicians like Dr. John Dee (astrologer to Queen Elizabeth I), the Occult tradition has explored the magick of conjuring spirits, divination through ceremonial practices, and other practices designed to increase humankind's knowledge and mastery of the spiritual realm. Unlike Wicca, descended primarily from the wise woman tradition of European shamanism, the roots of ceremonial magick lie more in the academic world of priests, philosophers, and alchemists. While Wicca functions primarily as a magickal system of folk spirituality and healing, ceremonial magick functions primarily as a system of mastery and control over humankind's spiritual destiny.

In general, the rituals of ceremonial magicians tend to be much more intricate, deeply symbolic and astrologically fine-tuned than those performed by Witches. Although some Wiccans do employ a considerable amount of ceremonial magick in their rites, many others prefer to keep their rituals very simple.

Despite all of their differences, it would be a mistake to suggest Wicca and ceremonial Occultism have nothing in common. Many Witches, from Gerald Gardner to the present day, have also been ceremonialists. Like Wiccans, ceremonial magicians draw inspiration from Pagan mythology and Goddess religion. Much of the occult knowledge taught by Wiccan elders comes out of the ceremonial tradition.

The word occult literally means hidden (for example, a medical occult blood test is a procedure looking for hidden blood). Therefore, the Occult tradition involves the transmission of hidden wisdom. Why has this wisdom been hidden? Partially because of the persecution that magick has occasionally undergone at the hand of organized religion, but also because of the conviction among magicians that the true power of magickal principles needs to be revealed to the student in a gradual, supervised process. Magick involves deep processes of psychological transformation, and as such needs to be pursued in a careful and safe way. For this reason, most books on magickal theory and practice contain only the most basic of exercises that individuals can safely perform without supervision.

The books profiled in this chapter focus primarily on the Occult tradition of ceremonial magick. Included here are a few old texts, some dating back several centuries, as well as histories of the modern Occult along with workbooks for the modern student. While many Wiccans would prefer to leave the fancy rituals alone and just want to go out and gather herbs, others will find useful insights into the practice of magick in the history and exercises found in these books.

Manly P. Hall
The Secret Teaching of All Ages
(An Encyclopedic Outline of Masonic, Hermetic,
Qabbalistic and Rosicrucian Symbolical Philosophy, Being
an Interpretation of the Secret Teachings concealed within
the Rituals, Allegories and Mysteries of All Ages), Diamond
Jubilee Edition

Originally published in the 1920s, this magisterial book contains a lifetime's worth of esoteric teachings, from the main traditions of Western Occultism (with a bit of Islamic and Native American lore thrown in for good measure). From ancient Egypt through to the flowering of alchemy and mysticism in the Middle Ages, up to the golden age of Occultism and magick in the 18th and 19th centuries, the material contained herein will thrill the seeker after the higher mysteries with its sheer breadth and depth.

Anthony Aveni
Behind the Crystal Ball: Magic, Science, and the Occult
From Antiquity Through the New Age

Colin Wilson
The Occult: A History

Two comprehensive histories of the western inner tradition. Aveni's work considers the often-troubled relationship between magick and science, while Wilson defines magick as "the science of the future" and considers the history of this topic in terms of the human quest for unleashing the powers of consciousness.

Samuel Liddell MacGregor Mathers, translator
The Goetia: The Lesser Key of Solomon the King (Clavicula Salomonis Regis), edited with an introduction by Aleister Crowley, illustrated second edition

The 20th-century edition of an English-language grimoire that dates back to the 16th century. The text includes instructions on conjuring spirits, creating a magick circle, the use of magickal seals, invocations of the Elements, and various other magickal practices. An interesting glimpse into the history of magick, both in terms of the grimoire itself, as well as its celebrated translator (one of the founders of the Golden Dawn) and editor (probably the most notorious ceremonial magician of the 20th century).

Francis Barrett
The Magus: A Complete System of Occult Philosophy

Another classic work of ritual magick, compiling occult information from a variety of sources, making many texts available in English for the first time ever. The book covers topics such as natural magick, alchemy, numerology, astrology, talismanic magick, the Kabbalah and ceremonial magick; the final section includes biographies of famous magicians including John Dee and Albertus Magnus.

Dennis William Hauck
The Emerald Tablet: Alchemy for Personal Transformation

According to legend, the original emerald tablet contained the alchemical formula necessary to change base metals into gold. The lore surrounding this mythic tablet is central to the grand western esoteric tradition of alchemy, which uses the quest to turn base metals into gold as a metaphor for the spiritual transformation of the body and soul and for the quest for eternal life. The dynamics of such a spiritual quest are given fresh life through this accessible yet profound study by Hauck, a transpersonal psychologist who is himself a practicing alchemist. For Wiccans who desire to weave the deepest streams of western Hermeticism into their magickal practice, this book provides an overview of the riches available to the earnest seeker.

R. J. Stewart
The Underworld Initiation: A Journey Toward Psychic Transformation

Like many masterpieces of Western Occultism, this book is at times dense, abstract, and nearly impenetrable. But the reader gets a sense of the author's profound knowledge and, by the end, will have received a compelling glimpse of the magickal reality of other worlds. Stewart looks at oral tradition, Celtic myth and legend, and the esoteric symbolism surviving in folk songs to introduce the reader to the means of otherworld contact as preserved in the western mystery tradition.

Franz Bardon
Initiation into Hermetics: The Path of the True Adept

The theory and practice of magick, examining the magick of the Elements, the Akasha or Etheric body, and the various planes of human existence, before providing in-depth instruction and exercises in the magickal schooling of the spirit, the soul, and the physical body. Includes exercises in psychic skills (from clairvoyance to telepathy), astral travel, and Elemental ritual work.

Israel Regardie
The Complete Golden Dawn System of Magic

Ten volumes of detailed information on the rituals, teachings, and practices of the Golden Dawn tradition of magick, published here in a gigantic single-volume edition. Combining mysticism grounded in the Kabbalistic Tree of Life and the

Hebrew alphabet, with Egyptian mythology and symbolism; featuring meditative exercises, consecrations, and other rituals, this densely packed omnibus probably contains more information than you'll probably ever need on this influential system.

Donald Michael Kraig
Modern Magick, Eleven Lessons in the High Magical Arts, Second edition

A clearly organized step-by-step introduction to ceremonial magick, useful even for the utter beginner. Lots of information that can be collaterally useful to Wiccans, from detailed instructions on the Lesser Banishing Ritual of the Pentagram (a tool for psychic self-defense) to insight into the Kabbalah, Tarot, Elemental magick, and astral travel.

John Michael Greer
Inside a Magical Lodge: Group Ritual in the Western Tradition

Instead of providing the detailed instructions in magick similar to the work of Donald Michael Kraig or Israel Regardie, this book considers magick in terms of the lodge, or magickal fraternity. Topics covered include the history of magickal lodges, along with customs of lodges, practical matters (like elections and administration), and the inner work of such bodies.

Dion Fortune
The Mystical Qabalah

First published in the 1930s, this masterpiece by one of England's best known occultists takes the mystical Jewish tradition of Qabalah (or Kabbalah) and presents it in a way that makes its teaching and symbolism relevant to the modern esoteric seeker. Many Wiccans resist using the Qabalah as a spiritual tool because of its connection with patriarchal religion. But writers like Fortune (as well as Ellen Cannon Reed, whose Wiccan book on the Qabalah is profiled in Chapter 8) assert that Qabalistic symbolism represents a universal mysticism that can be applied to any positive religious or spiritual path.

Robert Anton Wilson
Cosmic Trigger, Volume I: Final Secret of the Illuminati

Not a book on magick or Occultism as such, but important because it explores non-ordinary reality and the potential of human consciousness to be amazed by the experiences found in mind-corridors off the beaten path of consensus reality. Wilson takes a hard look at conspiracy theories, psychedelic drugs, and the psychology of paranoia, all important topics for magicians (and Witches) to understand. Magick can open the mind to some really bizarre stuff. Wilson's perspective can help the student of magick to remain centered.

— Part Three —
Wicca in the Real World

Okay. You've read the basics, and you've been exploring the various elements of the Craft; at least those that particularly speak to you. Now what? Where does Wicca lead, beyond ever deeper explorations of myth, symbol, and ritual?

Witches heal and Witches work magick. As change agents, catalysts of transformation in a world desperately in need of love and compassion, Witches can bring healing to the world not only through ritual and magick, but also by fostering mental, psychological, communal, sexual, and ecological well-being. In subtle but important ways, Wiccans transform society by embracing new perspectives on topics ranging from history to science to gardening. Witches may even foster healing through art, music, or literature, whether as artists themselves or by simply enjoying the magickal efforts of others.

Such practical application of Craft wisdom forms the basis for the remainder of this book. In one way or another, the books profiled in the chapters to come foster healing, wellness, and transformation. These books can inspire those who love the old ways to reach out to others, in perfect love and perfect trust—thereby changing the world forever, and for the better. This ultimately is the magick of the Craft.

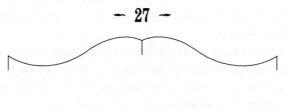

27

HISTORY FOR
WITCHES

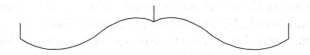

To understand Wicca's place in the real world, let's begin by gaining a sense of history. To do that, we need to study not only Wiccan history, but Pagan, magickal, and Goddess history as well. From a historical survey of Pagan Europe, to the sexual politics of "partnership" societies versus patriarchal "dominator" cultures, to the relationship between the development of written communication and the suppression of Goddess spirituality, each book here explores some aspect of history that can shed light on the ancient tradition of Nature religion and the contemporary explosion of Wiccan ways.

Modern Wiccan history can be understood as the history of a spirituality of protest. Wicca protests the patriarchal images of God-as-male-only, and the history of oppression against women that took its worst form in the European Witch hunts. Wicca protests sickness and brokenness in the world by providing healing to those who need it. In our time, Wicca protests the trashing of the planet in the name of human greed and laziness, calling for a renewed commitment to conservation and ecological healing.

Knowing history, whether specifically relevant to Witches or the general history of the human family, helps us understand how we got to the place we are today. Such knowledge empowers us to choose wisely for the future. Those who do not know history are doomed to repeat it, as the proverb maintains. Witches need to know Pagan history as well as the history of mainstream culture so that Wiccan spirituality may continue to move in the direction of healing and of devotion to the old ways.

One book mentioned here bears additional commentary: Linda Ellerbe's *The Dark Side of Christian History*. By including this book, I do not mean to gratuitously attack Christianity. On the contrary, I think Pagans need to refrain from useless Christian-bashing. Many Witches grew up Christian and consciously chose to leave that religion when they embraced the Craft. It's difficult to leave a religion, and so one strategy involves regarding Christianity as some sort of horrendously vile system of oppression. Such anti-Christian sentiments may help Witches feel justified in abandoning their childhood faith, but it does little to cultivate true healing in the world. In truth, Christianity (like any other institution) has many different sides, both beautiful and terrible. Wiccans gain far more by treating Christians with respect and honor than with anger and rejection. Remember, Wicca is the path of healing.

So why am I profiling such an inflammatory anti-Christian book, then? Well, I do believe Wiccans need a realistic understanding of Christianity; after all, most Witches interact with Christian friends and relatives every day. Many Wiccans face subtle and not-so-subtle pressure from Christians to submit to their religion. Having a balanced understanding of Christianity can help Wiccans maintain an adult commitment to magickal spirituality. For that matter, those who want to shape a positive future for Wicca need to understand the mistakes other religions have made—to avoid revisiting those same problems.

Margaret Murray
The Witch-Cult in Western Europe

Margaret Murray
The God of the Witches

Scholars now regard Murray's theories as flawed, but at one time her ideas literally changed how people understood Witch-craft. Murray asserted that the European Witch hunts involved the persecution of people who practiced a vestigial Pagan religion, an idea that led to new attitudes in our culture toward the burning times—clearing the way for the public emergence of the Craft. Before taking these ideas literally, read Hutton's *The Triumph of the Moon* (an important history book that was profiled in Chapter 9). Murray's books are useful mainly as reference works for understanding the intellectual history of Wicca.

Leonard Shlain
The Alphabet Versus the Goddess: the Conflict Between Word and Image

By combining neuroscience, archaeology, theology, philosophy, and cultural history, Leonard Shlain explores how changes in the way people communicate often coincide with spiritual revolutions. The rise of patriarchal monotheism coincided with the invention of the written alphabet. The burning times followed the invention of moveable type. The 20th-century renaissance of Goddess spirituality occurred simultaneously with the invention of video as a communication tool. Shlain argues that the millennia-old struggle between God and Goddess is, in many ways, influenced by changes in the ways human beings communicate.

Prudence Jones and Nigel Pennick
A History of Pagan Europe

A comprehensive study not only of pre-Christian European spirituality, but also of the many ways in which Pagan spirituality influenced and continues to influence European culture, which culminates in a consideration of the modern Pagan renaissance. The book examines all the major streams of indigenous European religion, including Classical (Greek and Roman), Celtic, Nordic, and Baltic forms of Paganism.

Heinrich Kramer and James Sprenger
The Malleus Maleficarum (The Witches' Hammer)

The 15th century manual, written by two Dominican priests, for identifying, hunting down, and destroying Witches. Even if most of the people who were killed in the European Witch hunts did not think of themselves as Pagans or Goddess worshipers, it is still a horrifying chapter in history, one in which a culture turned against its own women, killing them by the thousands. We must not forget that this book existed—and we need to work together to ensure this kind of thing never happens again.

Charles G. Leland
Etruscan Roman Remains

Originally published in 1892, this collection of folklore and legend was gathered by Charles Leland, who also translated and published *Aradia* (Chapter 8). Here are the words of 19th century Italian Witches, sorceresses, and wise women, expressing their devotion to the full moon and to Diana. An important source for modern Wicca's pre-Gardnerian roots.

Ralph Merrifield
The Archaeology of Ritual and Magic

An archaeological approach to the evidence for primitive ritual in pre-Christian Europe. The author considers how

ancient artifacts point toward such practices as making offer-
ings to earth and water spirits, spells for psychic self-defense,
and funeral rites. In examining ritual practices throughout the
ages, the author discovers that modern humankind has more in
common with our ancestors then we might realize.

Carlo Ginzburg
Ecstasies: Deciphering the Witches' Sabbath

Ginzburg looks at the question of the Witches' Sabbath,
the alleged meeting of Witches that inquisitors usually extracted
from those who were accused of practicing Witchcraft. Instead
of looking for evidence of an organized cult, Ginzburg suggests
that ancient Pagan religion was shamanistic in nature, and considers the similarities between shamanistic practices and the
allegations made against accused Witches.

Riane Eisler
The Chalice and the Blade: Our History, Our Future

Influential but controversial consideration of the theory that
European culture at one point seemed shaped by egalitarian,
nonviolent values, before being run over by Indo-European
invaders who brought a patriarchal mindset into the lands they
conquered. For some Wiccans, this vision of the past is an inspiration to work for a similarly idyllic future; but others might
find it easier to believe Cynthia Eller's version of history (see
the following).

Cynthia Eller
The Myth of Matriarchal Prehistory: Why an Invented Past Won't Give Women a Future

Once upon a time, did men and women live together in a
blissful, nonviolent, egalitarian society of Goddess-worshipers?
Many feminist writers, like Marija Gimbutas and Riane Eisler,

have argued as much. But others, like Cynthia Eller, have questioned whether the evidence really supports such a view of the past. Not only does this book challenge the matriarchal theory of history, but it explains why such a theory isn't necessarily helpful for women (and men) who are trying to create a more balanced society today.

Valerie I. J. Flint
The Rise of Magic in Early Medieval Europe
The author traces the history of Christian attitudes toward magick in the so-called Dark Ages (roughly 500-1100 C.E.), showing how church authorities were not always hostile toward magick, but tolerated it and even assimilated non-Christian magickal practices into Christian ceremonies. Such a liberal attitude strengthened, rather than weakened, the church's role in society. In later years a more conservative attitude prevailed, but this book suggests the relationship between magick and official religion was not always strained.

Helen Ellerbe
The Dark Side of Christian History
A helpful resource for anyone who wants to develop a balanced understanding of a religion that too often promotes itself as the agent of God and therefore, is above criticism. Pagans, whose beliefs are based in Nature, know that everything has a dark side. In looking at the Inquisition, the persecution of Jews and Muslims, the killing of Witches, and other noncommendable episodes in church history, this book enables the reader to view the Christian church objectively and fairly.

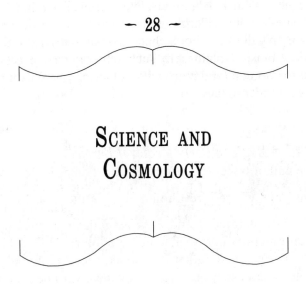

SCIENCE AND COSMOLOGY

Science and religion have not always been the best of friends. The Catholic church tried to suppress Galileo's discoveries about the nature of the solar system, while Darwin's theories of evolution have met with stiff opposition from Protestant fundamentalists. It seems that religion governs questions of personal meaning and faith about a future beyond death, while science examines practical matters of knowledge about the physical universe. And never the twain shall meet.

Because most religions derive their authority from a book—a set of sacred writings—they must suppress any ideas or theories that compete with the message of their sacred book. Religions based on the written word eventually become constricted by orthodoxy, dogmatism, and the suppression of "heresies." But science, as the human quest for knowledge of the universe, moves forward by questioning the existing way of looking at things. Religions of the written word naturally foster dogmatism, while science (at least in theory) challenges any and all dogma that stand in the way of knowledge. No wonder there's conflict here.

Wicca looks to Nature, rather than a body of sacred writings, as its source for authority. When Pagans and Witches look for answers in life, they turn not to a Bible or other book, but to the silent wisdom of the universe itself. Of course, Wiccans rely on books as records of humankind's efforts to understand the natural world. But because no book has the stamp of ultimate authority, no revolution in science can be suppressed as heresy. On the contrary, Paganism fosters intellectual freedom, where a revolution in scientific thought can be welcomed as a new way to love and revere the Goddess in her physical form. Many Witches are keen scientists, finding in their research the same sense of wonder that they also find in ritual and meditation.

I don't mean to imply that every scientist and Wiccan in the world innately agree on everything. Empirically-minded scientists might take issue with Paganism's acceptance of reincarnation, psychic healing, and mystical experience, and Pagans might find the skepticism of such empiricists to be in its own odd way a kind of rigid orthodoxy. But these kinds of intellectual disagreement involve not the violation of dogma, but simply the creative conflict that comes when different ways of interpreting the world collide. Wicca values imagination, inner experience, and the wisdom of intuition, meditation, dreams, and visions. Some scientists reject such things as inconsequential, but recent developments in quantum physics have resulted in a new humility in the scientific world. Witches often have much in common with the researcher who realizes that mysticism just might be an important source of knowledge for understanding the atom.

The following list includes books of imaginative and, in some cases, speculative science that resonates deeply with the magickal world-view held by many Witches. Some titles explore cosmological questions of interest to Wiccans (such as the possibility of reincarnation). Witches believe in a magickal, wondrous, mystical universe, but it's a universe that can be known and at least partially understood. Science represents our quest to achieve such understanding.

J. E. Lovelock
Gaia: A New Look at Life On Earth

Consider the earth as a system in which all forms of life and the Elements of the biosphere work together for the collective good. Life on earth arises from some sort of unified system dedicated to preserving, cultivating, and enhancing the evolutionary process of life. According to this view, all life on earth participates in this unified system—Gaia—in a manner similar to how billions of cells each play a part in forming one human being. As a scientist, not a mystic, Lovelock carefully avoids the spiritual potential of his ideas, but Pagans find it easy to integrate his ideas into the cosmology of Nature religion.

Fred Alan Wolf, Ph.D.
Mind into Matter: A New Alchemy of Science and Spirit

Alchemy has been a powerful symbol for metaphysicians and magicians who seek to unlock the mystery of creation through attempts to transform base metals into gold (a metaphor for transforming the ordinary human soul into divine consciousness). Wolf, a leading scientist whose work explores the modern re-connection between physics and metaphysics, here considers how the ancient traditions of alchemy can contribute to the present and future integration of science and spirit.

Ken Wilber
A Brief History of Everything

This book, written in an interview-like question and answer format, summarizes the ideas in Wilber's magisterial

Sex, Ecology, Spirituality. Challenging both the otherworldly strains of spirituality that view only the realm of spirit as important, as well as the scientific mind that regards any talk of spirituality as hogwash, Wilber depicts a holistic model of the universe (and of human knowledge) where the inner and outer worlds are equally important and equally necessary fields of inquiry.

Joseph Head and S. L. Cranston, editors
Reincarnation: The Phoenix Fire Mystery
My copy of this book has the following description on the cover: "An east-west dialogue on death and rebirth from the worlds of religion, science, psychology, philosophy, art, and literature, and from the great thinkers of the past and present," which handily sums up the focus of the anthology. This book explores the idea of reincarnation from just about every conceivable angle. Almost a fourth of the book contains excerpts from the writing of scientists who accepted, or at least considered, the possibility of soul recycling.

Mark B. Woodhouse
Paradigm Wars: Worldviews for a New Age
In many ways, New Age science represents a major cosmological revolution in how humankind understands the world and our place in it. Woodhouse's book considers the tension between "old age" and New Age science, exploring alternative medicine, holistic education, spiritual healing, ecofeminism, reincarnation, and new physics—topics of interest to many in the Wiccan community. As an academic, Woodhouse brings a balanced critical eye to this encyclopedic survey of cutting-edge ideas.

Fritjof Capra
The Tao of Physics, Third edition, updated

Fritjof Capra
The Turning Point: Science, Society, and the Rising Culture

Two visionary works of science and culture, both of which explore how integrating science and spirituality may lead to a transformation in human knowledge. Although *The Tao of Physics* inspired numerous other science-meets-mysticism books, perhaps the most important element of Capra's message may be found in *The Turning Point*—that humankind needs to embrace a philosophical and political approach to life based on the principles of the new physics, thereby replacing the old mechanistic model of life with a new, organic, systems-oriented vision.

Michael S. Schneider
A Beginner's Guide to Constructing the Universe: The Mathematical Archetypes of Nature, Art and Science

A fun, educational, and usefully illustrated tour through the physics of numbers, looking at how numeric values (from one to 10) illuminate our knowledge of the natural order. DNA, the I Ching, and sacred geometry all contribute to this innovative way of understanding science.

Michio Kaku
Hyperspace: A Scientific Odyssey Through Parallel Universes, Time Warps, and the 10th Dimension

Douglas R. Hofstadter
Gödel, Escher, Bach: an Eternal Golden Braid, A Metaphorical Fugue on Minds and Machines in the Spirit of Lewis Carroll.

Stephen Hawking
The Illustrated Brief History of Time

These best-selling books on cutting-edge science demonstrate just how weird things have gotten on the frontier of human knowledge. Prepare for your mind to be bent and stretched in fascinating new ways.

Robert Lawlor
Sacred Geometry: Philosophy and Practice

Illustrations, mathematical formulae, and geometric diagrams combine with the author's narrative to introduce the esoteric approach to mathematics and geometry. Combining a history of sacred geometry with practical exploration of the mathematical approach to spiritual wisdom, this book makes an arcane topic easily accessible.

Hamish Miller and Paul Broadhurst
The Sun and the Serpent: An Investigation into Earth Energies

The authors combine their expertise as a dowser and a photographer to explore a leyline—a line of earth energy, marked by a number of sacred and prehistoric sites along the track—in the southwestern English region of Cornwall. Their exploration not only serves as a travelogue for that part of England, but also as a meditation on the mystical understanding of the earth as a living being whose energy becomes visible to humans along the leys.

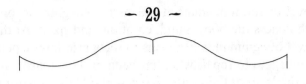

29

PSYCHOLOGY AND COMMUNITY

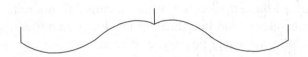

The classic stereotype of the Witch involves an old hag who lives by herself, deep in the woods, stirring yucky things into her cauldron as she waits for little children to come along so that she might eat them. She is isolated, anti-social, and basically foul-tempered.

Like most stereotypes of Witches, this one has little bearing on reality. Wiccans are mostly gregarious folks who enjoy a good party. Many do have a solitary streak in them; indeed, Wicca as a spiritual path honors solitary practice as a valid option for honoring the old ways. But whether a Witch prefers to cast her circle alone or with others, her craft ultimately involves serving others, for it involves healing. Healing, after all, doesn't happen in a vacuum.

In their book *The Cultural Creatives*, Paul H. Ray and Sherry Ruth Anderson say this about healing:

To heal means to wake up to our true nature. At the level of the individual, it means to recognize as one wholeness the body, mind, emotion, and spirit. At the level of community, it means to recognize interdependence and to repair what has been broken apart. And at the level of the earth, to heal—the Hebrew word is tikkun—means to call home those who have been in exile, to redeem and bring peace to our world (194).

This holistic and communal view of healing arises from core spiritual truths, such as the Buddhist concept of "interbeing" (as put forth by Thich Nhat Hanh) or the Lakota concept of *mitakuye owasin*, which means "all my relations." Wiccans understand how healing involves community issues; drug abuse, violence, poverty, and crime are not only someone else's problems, but truly affect all those who share a common life. Healing involves environmental issues, not only for the sake of the earth herself, but also out of recognition that a trashed ecosystem cannot effectively support our physical health or the well-being of our children. Ultimately, the healing dimension of Wicca involves far more than just reiki and herbs. It involves a commitment to the environment, a commitment to healthy relationships, and a commitment to fostering wellness for all.

This is the first of three chapters that explore the more global applications of healing, specifically in terms of community and psychology, gender and sexuality, and Nature and the environment. Each of these topics involves areas of life where people experience pain and suffering. Witches may not be able to solve all the problems in the world, but we can certainly use our healing skills to alleviate some of the hurt.

The books profiled in this chapter fall under two broad categories: psychology and community-building. Psychological health supports the healing of communities (and vice versa).

As for community itself, the books presented here all contribute in one way or another to healing, either of Wiccan community, or of the larger social and political communities in which Wiccans live.

Psychology

Carl G. Jung
The Essential Jung: Selected Writings

Witches from Janet and Stewart Farrar to Vivianne Crowley have acknowledged their indebtedness to Jung, one of the towering giants of 20th-century psychology. His investigations into the psychology of the unconscious, ritual, symbolism, dreams, alchemy, and the Occult, prove extremely useful to those who wish to understand the dynamics of the mind in relation to spirituality. This book collects key writings from Jung's vast body of work, making it the perfect introductory text.

Daniel Goleman
Emotional Intelligence

Recognizing that emotional skills like self-awareness, self-discipline, and empathy play as important a role in life as does sheer brainpower, Goleman argues that we should measure intelligence on an emotional, as well as a mental, scale. He provides insight on how parents can help nurture emotional intelligence in their children. Given that Wicca is a spiritual path devoted to healing and to holistic living, this book provides a roadmap to Witches who want to balance their thinking ability with feeling skills.

Brad Blanton, Ph.D.
Radical Honesty: How to Transform Your Life By Telling the Truth

A controversial psychology of finding health and happiness by letting go of deception, in whatever form it may take in our lives. Blanton points out how much mental (and physical) illness arises out of our basic unwillingness to be honest with ourselves, our spouses, our bosses, and others to whom we relate. A book with both personal and social ramifications, it promises to liberate us from the jail of moralism—a freedom similar to what Witchcraft affirms in the Wiccan Rede. If it harms none, do what you will. Just don't lie about it.

Theodore Roszak, Mary E. Gomes, and Allen D. Kanner, editors
Ecopsychology: Restoring the Earth, Healing the Mind

Essays by psychologists and ecologists, coming together to explore how mental and environmental health depend on each other. Ironically, the section called "Political Engagement" has the material of most immediate interest to Wiccans, with essays on the ecopsychology of the Goddess and of magick.

Community

Arnold Mindell
Sitting in the Fire: Large Group Transformation Using Conflict and Diversity

A courageous and powerful blueprint for managing and healing conflict. The basic premise of this book is that diversity happens, and that it's a good thing. But often people who have more power because of cultural privilege will, consciously or not, abuse or otherwise disempower those who lack privilege. Our society tends to ignore issues of privilege, prejudice, and power, so these concerns often make us feel uncomfortable.

But if we ignore the forces that undermine community, we will fail in our attempts to create lasting community—whether we're talking about a community of three or three hundred million. Mindell's work is not easy, comfortable reading, but that's part of why it is so essential.

Dudley Weeks, Ph.D.
The Eight Essential Steps to Conflict Resolution: Preserving Relationships at Work, at Home, and in the Community

The subtitle of this book points out the importance of resolving conflict: it is the key to preserving relationships. In this sense, conflict resolution is a form of healing. This book outlines a simple process of transforming hostile, tense relationships that are strained by conflict into "conflict partnerships" where the warring parties affirm their common goals in successfully reconciling. Like *Sitting in the Fire*, this is an essential text for any Wiccan leader, both in terms of keeping the peace in a coven, but also empowering Wiccans to deal with conflict as it erupts with non-Wiccans.

Kenneth C. Haugk
Antagonists in the Church: How to Identify and Deal With Destructive Conflict

Endorsed by prominent Pagans like Isaac Bonewits, this is a book written for Christian leaders, complete with Christian theology and Biblical references. But its value to Wiccans lies in its universal message: Any kind of spiritual organization can (and alas, usually does) suffer from antagonists—people who bring energies of discord, chaos, and sabotage to the community. While conflict is a normal part of any social group and can be a creative force for necessary change, antagonists are those people who create conflict that can actually harm and undermine the community. Pagans are no better than anyone else, and so our groups have their own share of antagonists. This book, written for spiritual leaders, identifies the typical behavior of antagonistic persons, along with practical advice for dealing with those whose energy is destructive rather than creative.

Starhawk
Dreaming the Dark: Magic, Sex and Politics

Starhawk
Truth or Dare, Encounters with Power, Authority, and Mystery

The author of *The Spiral Dance* explores the relationship between political activism and spirituality. Her understanding of Wicca emphasizes feminism and environmentalism as sources of meaning and value. *Dreaming the Dark* celebrates the ways in which spiritual community and ritual can nurture those on the political front line, while *Truth or Dare* examines different forms of power: power-over-others, power-from-within, and power-with, using the myth of Inanna to envision healthier models for human relations. Starhawk's views have been embraced by many within the Nature spirituality movement, even though some (notably Ellen Cannon Reed) argue against making Wicca too political.

Carole Kammen and Jodi Gold
Call to Connection: Bringing Sacred Tribal Values into Modern Life

The "sacred tribal values" promoted by this book include belonging, recognition, ritual, education, service, trust and faith, and completing the circle. Sound familiar? Many of the values mainstream society yearns for are actively practiced by Pagan groups. This book explores how such traditional values can be integrated into our culture as a whole.

Christina Baldwin
Calling the Circle: The First and Future Culture
Another call for the integration of primal cultural values into contemporary society; this book celebrates the concept of the circle as the model for nonhierarchical, cooperative, consensus-based communities and relationships. A powerful new vision of society grounded in the most basic element of Nature spirituality.

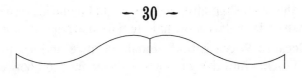

30

THE BODY:
GENDER AND SEXUALITY

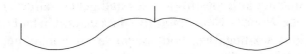

Wicca is a fertility religion.

The Goddess and the God are juicy, passionate lovers; indeed, the Goddess proclaims, "All acts of love and pleasure are my rituals." The central ritual act of the Craft, the Great Rite, involves the sacred erotic union of lover and beloved.

Simply put, Nature spirituality regards sexuality as holy and sex itself as basically good, even if sometimes expressed poorly or in harmful ways.

Wicca attempts to maintain this sex-positive spirituality while operating in a culture deeply conflicted over sexuality. Mass media assaults us with images of sexy people, mostly presented on the level of adolescent titillation and cynically designed to arouse consumers. Meanwhile, although many alternative sexual lifestyles thrive in modern life (from gay and lesbian communities to polyamorists and the "lifestyle," or swinging community), many people still rigidly cling to Victorian ideas that sex is dirty, the body shameful, and any sexual behavior outside the most strict boundaries of male-female marriage is taboo.

Because Wicca is both female-positive and sex-positive, most Witches intuitively recognize the connection between the suppression of sexuality and the oppression of women. Societal messages like "Sex is dirty" and "Obey your husbands" seem to come from the same deep wound in our collective psyche. To heal one requires the healing of both.

Thankfully, modern society is slowly redefining the ways in which men and women relate and share power. Meanwhile, we struggle to redefine our attitudes toward sexuality. But the mix of conflicting attitudes toward sex and gender affects everyone, even Witches. Newcomers to Wicca may often harbor subconscious sex-negative, body-negative, or female-negative beliefs. Witches, like everyone else, need to sort through the confused and conflicting attitudes of mainstream culture to be true to the principles of the old religion.

The books profiled in this chapter do not all agree with one another and do not necessarily reflect the feelings of all (or even most) Wiccans. Some subjects covered here, like polyamory or sacred prostitution, may not be to everyone's liking. My intention is not to endorse any one sexual lifestyle, but to celebrate diversity. The common thread uniting these titles is the radical commitment to the goodness of eros.

If it harms none, do what you will. What sets Wicca apart from nearly all other spiritual paths is the freedom and openness in which adults can responsibly explore different options for the healthy expression of sexuality. Whether Wiccans live in traditional heterosexual marriages or adopt a non-mainstream sexual lifestyle, their sexuality remains blessed by a spiritual path rooted in Nature.

In affirming sexuality as sacred, a few of the books profiled here explore Tantra or sexual magick. Others, however, take a more political approach. Redefining sexuality as good needs to happen not only on the personal level, but on the public, communal level as well. And finally I've mentioned a few books that explore ecofeminism, a topic that links this chapter to the next.

Special note to young readers: Sorry, but these books are not yet appropriate for you. Wicca not only stands for sexual freedom, but also for responsibility that comes with maturity. Save this chapter for later—your day will come.

Riane Eisler
Sacred Pleasure: Sex, Myth, and the Politics of the Body— New Paths To Power and Love

A sweeping overview of the history of sexual politics. Once upon a time, sex was sacred and spirituality had an erotic element. With the rise of what Eisler calls the "dominator world," the union of sex and spirit was rent. Naturally, Eisler calls for a return to a pleasure-based culture of sexuality.

Julie Henderson
The Lover Within: Opening to Energy in Sexual Practice

Henderson provides over 70 practical exercises for solo or couple work, covering such embodied processes as breathing, visualization, relaxation, and emotional release. These exercises can help loosen the emotional armoring we carry in our bodies, thereby improving the energy flow within sexual experience and opening sexuality up to deeper spiritual experience. Henderson points out that sexual energy work actually enables energy to flow within the body outside the bedroom as well.

Brandy Williams
Ecstatic Ritual: Practical Sex Magic

The Great Rite—the sacred union of lover and beloved—embodies the pinnacle of Craft ritual. But how does a couple go about practicing sexual magick? What are the necessary exercises for preparing to enact the Great Rite? This little book of magickal exercises provides a concise and useful introduction to one of the most mysterious aspects of Pagan spirituality. Read it with your beloved, and do the exercises.

Margo Anand
The Art of Sexual Ecstasy: The Path of Sacred Sexuality for Western Lovers

Another doorway into the higher mysteries of magickal sexuality, written from a Tantric perspective but in a way designed to benefit western readers. The book is full of great exercises designed not only to foster eyeball-popping sex, but (more importantly) to facilitate intimacy, love, and the clear flow of energy between the lovers' bodies.

Sirona Knight
Moonflower: Erotic Dreaming with the Goddess

The book includes 13 meditations on the eternal love between the God and the Goddess, arranged according to the lunar cycles of the year. Knight provides background information on the Goddess and the God for each month, along with a guided journey that two lovers can share as they invoke the energies of the deities into their own bedroom. A fun way for a couple to energize their lovemaking with Wiccan magick, month after month.

Nik Douglas and Penny Slinger
Sexual Secrets: The Alchemy of Ecstasy, 20th Anniversary Edition

The *Kama Sutra* meets *The Joy of Sex*. The Eastern tradition of sacred sexuality, presented in a practical, user-friendly, here's-how-you-do-it format. This book distills the wisdom of sages and mystic masters, making esoteric sexuality truly accessible for Westerners. Wonderfully illustrated with over 600 images—if possible, get the anniversary edition, for it includes many pictures in color.

Deborah Anapol, Ph.D.
Polyamory, The New Love Without Limits: Secrets of Sustainable Intimate Relationships

Ever wonder what became of the free love/open marriage movement of the 1960s? Well, here it is. Polyamory means "many loves" and refers to a variety of sexual and relationship styles, based on the idea that it's okay to love more than one person simultaneously. This isn't exactly swinging, which does not necessarily involve love. Nor is it about having an affair. Polyamory involves honest, ethical, relationship-oriented alternatives to the traditional twosome. While monogamy remains the norm for most Witches, some do practice open or group marriages, and even see the sex-positive and feminist-friendly qualities of Nature spirituality as especially supportive of polyamory.

Arthur Evans
Witchcraft and the Gay Counterculture: A Radical View of Western Civilization and Some of the People It Has Tried to Destroy

Evans explores the powerful (and often ignored) link between Nature spirituality and same-sex love. From considering the acceptance of homosexuality and bisexuality in shamanic societies to the cross-fertilization between the modern Wiccan community and the Gay, Lesbian, and Minority Sexuality communities, this book applauds the convergence between outlaw sexuality and outlaw religion.

Kenneth Ray Stubbs, editor
Women of the Light: The New Sexual Healers

From Mari Magdalene to the priestesses of Freya, women have incorporated sexuality into their capacity as priestesses and healers—and have been attacked for doing so by patriarchal detractors, who have labeled them as whores and harlots. This brave collection of personal stories reclaims the beauty and power of the sexual healer. Some of the women who contributed to this anthology are sexworkers, while others are artists, therapists, and teachers.

Rufus C. Camphausen
The Encyclopedia of Sacred Sexuality: From Aphrodisiacs and Ecstasy to Yoni Worship and Zap-lam Yoga

A delectable feast of sexy words, ideas, practices, and illustrations from the world's wisdom traditions. From sexy Gods and Goddesses to erotic scriptures such as the *Kama Sutra*, this work marshals all the evidence you'll ever need to understand just how deeply eroticism and spirituality converge.

Robert Lawlor
Earth Honoring: the New Male Sexuality

A lovely meditation on transforming male sexuality from locker room bravado to a much more compassionate, spiritually aware, and ecologically sensitive style of loving. Men who engage in ritual and who express sexuality in sacred ways are also men who know how to love and honor Nature, Mother Earth, and women.

Irene Diamond and Gloria Feman Orenstein, editors
Reweaving the World: The Emergence of Ecofeminism

Noël Sturgeon
Ecofeminist Natures: Race, Gender, Feminist Theory and Political Action

Carol J. Adams
Ecofeminism and the Sacred

Healing the body means healing the world and in turn means healing the relationship between men and women. Ecofeminist politics and spirituality explore the points of unity between these different areas of concern, and each of these books provides an intelligent introduction to the integration of environmentalist and feminist perspectives. See Chapter 31 for more on the spirituality of Nature and the land.

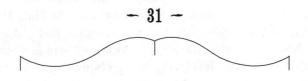

31

THE EARTH: NATURE, ECOLOGY, AND THE SACRED LAND

Healing our communities and healing our sexuality (the subjects of the last two chapters) naturally bring us to the largest and perhaps most important arena where healing needs to occur: the healing of the earth herself, of the natural environment in which we live. In a way, all of these forms of healing involve care of the body, understanding body in ever-larger ways. First, there is the actual body, in which we experience our sexuality and passion. Our bodies relate to others through the medium of community, which can be understood as a larger "body" of living beings. Finally, we have the "body" of the earth herself, the embodied presence of the Goddess through the natural world. The Christian church calls itself "the body of Christ." I think Witches ought to approach our community and our planet in a similar way, as "the body of the Goddess and the God."

When we think of the earth as the Goddess's body, we work within the cosmological framework of the Gaia Hypothesis (see Chapter 28). But this is more than just a dry scientific theory; honoring the body of Mother Earth is a blueprint for spiritual action. Just as the human body requires a balance of healthy diet, rest, and exercise, the body of Mother Earth requires balance. She requires rest from the incessant harvesting of her resources. She requires a diet of clean air, clean water, and protected rainforests. She requires the exercise of renewable energy sources, like solar and wind-generated power. Her body, like ours, will suffer if not treated adequately. Especially now that there are billions of human beings who rely on her, we must work harder than ever to insure her health and well-being.

As in the last two chapters, the books profiled here include both spiritually oriented titles as well as more politically or philosophically oriented works. For those who find mixing these kinds of books to be problematic, I'd like to make a statement for Wicca as a spiritual tradition where politics and community and spirituality do not need to be kept separate. Among many political activists there is a saying: "The personal is political." I think Pagans can adapt this to say, "The spiritual is political" and indeed, "The political is spiritual." This doesn't violate the separation of church and state, but rather seeks to integrate personal power with spiritual vision. Magick involves power; well, so does politics. A powerful magician can work wonders not only on the private level, but on the public level as well.

Therefore, the following books look at Nature in a variety of ways ranging from the strictly spiritual perspective of Colin Wilson, to the more political orientation of Susan Griffin, to the writing of Delores LaChappelle which integrates environmentalism and Nature spirituality to form a radical new vision. Not every Witch will agree with the ideas discussed in these books; but hopefully each title presented here can support, in some way, our efforts to heal the earth.

Jerry Mander
In the Absence of the Sacred: The Failure of Technology and the Survival of the Indian Nations

A withering critique of technology's role in modern life, and how our uncritical acceptance of technological "progress" has imperiled not only the natural world, but also the cultures of pre-industrial peoples. The author offers little hope for redemption in a world where technology increasingly dominates society, but looks to the fragile endurance of native peoples as hope for creating a future where technology exists in balance with humanity.

Melody
Love is in the Earth: A Kaleidoscope of Crystals, Updated edition

This guide to the energetic lore surrounding crystals is a treasure trove of information for anyone wishing to use minerals for magickal or alternative healing work. Melody writes out of a position of deep reverence for Mother Earth. Other "Love is in the Earth" titles by Melody include: *Mineralogical Pictorial, Laying-On-Of-Stones, Kaleidoscopic Pictorial Supplement A* and *Kaleidoscopic Pictorial Supplement Z*.

Paul Devereux
The Illustrated Encyclopedia of Ancient Earth Mysteries

A beautifully illustrated book that examines folklore, magickal spirituality, and unexplained phenomena related to the earth. The information included here can help Wiccans understand the relationship between Witchcraft and other primal or indigenous spiritual traditions, such as shamanism. Topics familiar to Witches (the Maypole, Fairies, and Stonehenge) are covered alongside information from other cultures (from the Aztecs to the Zuni).

Paul Devereux, John Steele, and David Kubrin
Earthmind: Tuning in to GAIA Theory with New Age Methods for Saving Our Planet

Devereux and his co-authors look at Gaia theory in relation to spirituality, the environmental crisis, and humankind's ongoing quest for meaning; the book culminates with suggestions on how individual human beings can cultivate their own share of earthmind, that is to say, of conscious identification with the mind of the Mother.

Nigel Pennick
Celtic Sacred Landscapes

Encounter the sacred sites of Europe through Celtic eyes. Pennick considers the spiritual, symbolic, and mythological dimension of the Celtic relationship to the land, through exploration of sites like Tintagel in Cornwall or Scelig Mihichil in Ireland; consideration of the sacred lore of trees, stones, and wells, and reflection on how the Celtic reverence for the land can revolutionize our culture today.

Rachel Pollack
The Body of the Goddess: Sacred Wisdom in Myth, Landscape, and Culture

Another exploration of the relationship between myth and the land, but focussed specifically on Goddess traditions. Pollack sees the land as the body of the Divine Feminine, and explores how ancient sites manifest that land-Goddess connection.

Jacqueline Memory Paterson
Tree Wisdom: The Definitive Guidebook to the Myth, Folklore and Healing Power of Trees

A British Druid priestess, Paterson combines the intense spirituality of her own deep immersion in the natural world with a thorough knowledge of the lore associated with trees indigenous to the British Isles (many of which also may be found in parts of North America). For each tree, Paterson provides botanical data, customs and legends surrounding the tree, along with magickal and healing information.

Shirley Nicholson and Brenda Rosen, compilers
Gaia's Hidden Life: The Unseen Intelligence of Nature

An anthology of writings on cultivating a conscious spiritual relationship with the earth. Includes essays representing different wisdom traditions, on topics such as the celebration of the living cosmos, the perspective of visionary science, shamanistic approaches to the natural world, and psychic/metaphysical encounters with Fairies and devas.

Cass Adams, editor
The Soul Unearthed: Celebrating Wildness and Personal Renewal Through Nature

Can the wilderness transform the spiritual seeker? The essays in this book explore the role of wildness and the wilderness in modern society. A defense of what is left of the wilderness, by celebrating its place as guardian of the depths of the human soul. To lose connection with the wilderness means losing touch with our own untamed, free selves. This book calls for renewing humanity's kinship with what lies beyond our control.

Elizabeth Roberts and Elias Amidon, editors
Earth Prayers From Around the World: 365 Prayers, Poems, and Invocations for Honoring the Earth

Poetic writings which honor the natural world and affirm the need for a holistic relationship with the earth. The meditations included in here come from many different spiritual traditions, cultures, and authors. A great gift book for all your non-Wiccan friends; here's a non-threatening way to invite others to experience the union of Spirit and Nature.

Susan Griffin
Woman and Nature: The Roaring Inside Her

A work of poetic prophecy, this feminist classic surveys the relationship between matter and mother (Latin: *mater*) as the essential key to understanding oppression. Sexist culture assumes that matter can be controlled because it is inert and passive; and since women, like Nature, represent matter (as opposed to the fatherly spirit), then women are to be ruled as surely as is Nature. Griffin laments the separations of man from woman and man from Nature, but nevertheless ends on a hopeful note as she considers the possibilities of reunion.

David Abram
The Spell of the Sensuous: Perception and Language in a More-Than-Human World

Hailed as a major work of ecological philosophy, this book weaves shamanistic ways of knowing into the author's investigations regarding the nature of language, the power of words to shape our sensory experience, and the importance of the non-human world (the natural wilderness) to provide our lives with meaning.

Dolores LaChappelle
Sacred Land, Sacred Sex, Rapture of the Deep: Concerning Deep Ecology and Celebrating Life

Radical ideas from one of the first women to be associated with the deep ecology movement. LaChappelle traces the history of humankind's split from Nature back to the philosophers of ancient Greece, up to the new world rip-off of modern capitalism. Through sacred sex, deep reverence for the land, and reconnection with ritual and other tribal values, we can begin to undo the damage that has been wreaked upon the Mother.

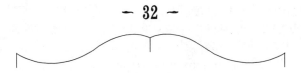

32

KITCHEN WITCHERY: GARDENING AND THE HOME

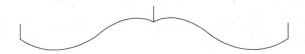

In Wicca, the kitchen wields as much power as the library—perhaps even more.

The spirituality of the Craft involves herbs and feasts as much as esoteric magick and ancient knowledge. A person can find happiness and fulfillment in Wicca through gardening, cooking, and managing a home, just as surely as through the study of mythology and lore. In a way, books, libraries, and academic scholarship represent the power of patriarchal knowledge; that is to say, the power of objective (as opposed to intuitive) reason. Not that there's anything wrong with books or with objective efforts to discover knowledge, but if that form of knowledge is regarded as the only way to learn wisdom and truth, then it has become imperious and has separated us from the innate deep wisdom of our bodies and our environment. So Wicca balances the bookish quest for knowledge by celebrating intuitive wisdom alongside empirical facts: the findings of psychics matter as much as the theories of physicists. In Goddess spirituality, theology arises not from academically trained scholars so much as from the common lore preserved by storytellers and folksingers.

So what does all this have to do with the kitchen? It is simple: In the kitchen, we find the wisdom of food, herbs, the garden, and the soil. In many ways, the kitchen (and by extension, the entire house and garden) is the laboratory in which we explore the science of Wicca. Whether it's through cooking a sumptuous feast in honor of the full moon, preparing an herbal salve to use in healing work, or fixing up a batch of fragrant incense for use in ritual and meditation, the work of the kitchen Witch is a central part of Nature-based spirituality.

Some of the books profiled in this chapter have an explicitly Wiccan or Pagan focus. Others don't have an obvious connection to Wicca, but contain information that Witches will find useful. Karen Kingston and Lilian Too provide two different approaches to feng shui, both of which can help readers to improve the flow of energy in their homes. *Laurel's Kitchen*, a classic vegetarian/natural foods cookbook, will help the kitchen Witch cook nutritious and yummy meals while staying in alignment with Wicca's commitment to the natural world.

Incidentally, the fact that I've included two vegetarian cookbooks does not mean I believe all Witches should be vegetarian. It's my bias, just as devoting an entire chapter to Celtic culture reflected by own preferences. Many Witches choose vegetarianism to honor the environment; after all, much of the clear-cutting of the rainforests in Latin America is happening to raise cattle for meat-hungry consumers in the United States. At any rate, I figured even the most ardent meat eaters can enjoy an occasional well-cooked vegetarian meal, so concentrating on meatless cookbooks seemed the way to go.

Scott Cunningham and David Harrington
The Magical Household: Empower Your Home With Love, Protection, Health, and Happiness

A simple overview of the many ways you can energize your living space with magick. Examining the home room by room, the authors provide spells, charms, recipes, as well as advice for plants and animals, furnishing, and observing the Wheel of the Year. A hands-on, practical guide to making magick an integral part of your life.

Patricia Telesco
A Kitchen Witch's Cookbook

Patricia Telesco
Gardening with the Goddess: Creating Gardens of Spirit and Magick

Patricia Telesco
A Witch's Beverages and Brews: Magick Potions Made Easy

Telesco describes herself as "a down-to-earth, militant Kitchen Witch" and her books reflect that sensibility, celebrating the crafty side of the Craft with lots of helpful information. *A Kitchen Witch's Cookbook* includes over 300 magickal recipes from around the world. *A Witch's Beverages and Brews* celebrates the history of medicinal beverages and magickal potions, and includes recipes arranged according to topics such as "Dreams and Meditation" and "Wisdom." *Gardening with the Goddess* provides delightful instruction on how to dedicate a garden (or part of one) to any of over 40 different Goddesses.

Lady Galadriel
The Magick of Incenses & Oils

Lady Galadriel
Magickal and Practical Scented Gifts

Two collections of recipes for incense, oils, salves, and various household herbal products. *Incenses & Oils* includes numerous ritual and spellcraft fragrances, along with more down-to-earth recipes for massage oils, perfumed unguents, and the like. *Scented Gifts* includes recipes for bath salts and soaps, potpourri, balms and lotions, and even a section on edible gifts. Basically, enough ideas in here to keep your magickal kitchen buzzing for months—if not years—to come.

Wylundt (Steven R. Smith)
Wylundt's Book of Incense
Why buy incense when you can make your own? This primer helps individuals to learn both about how to make incense as well as how to use it for magick in ritual. Over 350 recipes cover mundane, magickal, ritual, and planetary fragrances. Whether your favorite form of incense is as powder, cones, or sticks, Wylundt gives you directions for making your own.

Elizabeth Pepper and John Wilcock, editors
The Witches' Almanac
Billed as a "complete guide to lunar harmony," this is an almanac with a magical twist. Like other almanacs, it includes a calendar, planting and weather information, and various odds and ends. But it's written by and for Witches, so it combines a folksy New England design with a Wiccan sensibility.

Susan McClure
The Herb Gardener: A Guide for All Seasons
Did all the wonderful herbal books in Chapter 20 get you excited? This book will get you started on your own herbal garden, with tips on designing and starting the garden, along with information on the care of over 75 herbs.

Jim Knopf et al.
Natural Gardening: A Nature Company Guide

Out of love and reverence for the earth, Wiccans who garden try to keep their cultivated spaces as natural and organic as possible. This gorgeously illustrated book explores ways to blur the boundary between cultivation and wildness by creating a garden specifically to attract wildlife and otherwise let Nature take her course. Includes a list of plants especially well suited for natural gardening, divided by region in North America.

Peg Streep
Spiritual Gardening: Creating Sacred Space Outdoors

Another beautifully illustrated work, this book provides inspiration and practical ideas for creating a garden as a soul sanctuary. Includes "the tranquility garden," "the Gaia garden," "the Celtic garden," "the healing garden," and more.

Karri Allrich
Recipes from a Vegetarian Goddess: Delectable Feasts Through the Seasons

This collection of recipes playfully links vegetarian cuisine with Goddess spirituality, and arranges the entries according to the four seasons, making it easy for kitchen Witches to plan the perfect feast for each Sabbat. From "Winter Solstice Pumpkin Soup" to the "Eastern Goddess Summer Salad," there are lots of sumptuous delights to be found here.

Joanne Asala
Celtic Folklore Cooking

If you're going to honor the Celtic Gods and Goddesses in your rituals, then it only makes sense to honor them with the feast you serve afterward as well. This wonderful collection of recipes ties in folklore with many of the foods included here, enabling the Wiccan chef to choose items for a feast with specific magickal or mythological relevance.

Laurel Robertson, Carol Flinders, and Brian Ruppenthal
The New Laurel's Kitchen: A Handbook for Vegetarian Cookery & Nutrition

The grandmother of vegetarian cookbooks, filled not only with tantalizing recipes, but essential information on natural foods and nutrition for vegetarians. Even beyond that, it's a celebration of the kitchen, of the importance of taking the time to prepare wholesome and healthy meals—time our frenzied culture doesn't always allow us.

Lillian Too
Essential Feng Shui: A Step-by-Step Guide to Enhancing Your Relationships, Health and Prosperity

Feng shui applies Chinese metaphysical principles to home, garden, and workplace design, for the purpose of improving the flow of energy in the living space. This practical guidebook covers the basic principles of this ancient technique. As the title implies, the application of feng shui cures not only creates a more pleasant living space, but also can free up energy to allow love and money to flow more abundantly.

Karen Kingston
Clear Your Clutter With Feng Shui

Clutter blocks energy, and a cluttered living space can choke off the flow of magick. Karen Kingston mixes basic Feng Shui principles with good old-fashioned common sense in devising a spiritual approach to getting rid of clutter—and releasing the power of free-flowing energy.

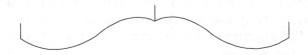

33

THE ARTS AND PERSONAL CREATIVITY

Among the ancient Celts, the spiritual leaders of the community fell into three broad categories: Druids, seers, and bards. As the priests and priestesses of the Celts, the Druids functioned as the philosophers, scientists, counselors, and judges, who officiated at sacred rites and taught the ancient lore. But there were also the seers, or ovates, the psychics and prophets who established contact with the spirits of the otherworld and who brought the wisdom of the spirit world back to the clan. And then the bards: the poets, harpists, and troubadours who kept the sacred memory of the people alive through stories and songs. An accomplished bard functioned almost like a shaman, for the words of a bard could magickally transport those who listened into the land where the Fairies dwelled.

Modern Wicca, like ancient Celtic spirituality, appreciates the distinctive spiritual power of priests and priestesses, psychics and diviners, and musicians and artists. Previous chapters have toured through priestly subjects like coven leadership or ritual design and the seer's work of psychic development and divination. Now, in this and the next two chapters, we come to the bardic functions of music, the arts, and literature, and their role within the Pagan spiritual journey.

Wicca has an inherent creative element. Consider the artistry involved in a kitchen Witch's work: making incenses, oils, herbal salves, and other crafty things. Also, since Wiccans take responsibility for setting up their own altars, writing their own rituals, and learning their own spells, even the ordinary practice of the old ways involves a dash of creativity. The bardic dimension of Witchcraft simply takes this natural creative element to the next level. People who have natural skills as musicians, storytellers, artists, seamstresses, or woodworkers, will find plenty of outlets for their talents within the practice of the old ways.

Chapters 34 and 35 focus specifically on creative writing: novels for adults and youth, as well as picture books for the children. Just as the ancient bards were gifted storytellers, so today a magickally-written novel or story can transport us to the otherworld. But in the present chapter, I'm focussing on books that call us to manifest our own creativity and excellence, as part of our spiritual journey. That's why I'm including "Personal Creativity" as part of this chapter, for developing creative skill can be a powerful way for a person to grow. Mainstream society often disempowers creativity: we celebrate the gifts of great geniuses like Mozart or Michelangelo, but then cut arts funding in our public schools so children are not given a chance to develop their own magnificence. Many adults go through life with a secret desire to make music or paint, but suppress such feelings as impractical. Wicca, however, can be a safe place for individuals to express their creativity, even if they are not geniuses or masters. The books profiled below either celebrate the creativity of others, or offer programs for you to develop your own artistic gifts.

Julia Cameron
The Artist's Way: A Spiritual Path to Higher Creativity

You don't need to be the kind of artist who draws or paints to benefit from the exercises and ideas found in this book, for its program is meant for enhancing creativity in the broadest possible sense, an effort that would benefit almost any endeavor, from business to parenting to, well, ritual magick. Cameron takes you on a journey through safety, identity, power, possibility, abundance, strength, compassion, and other creativity-enhancing concepts, always moving toward the nurturing (or recovery) of your innate magnificent artistry.

Gabriele Lusser Rico
Writing the Natural Way: Using Right-Brain Techniques to Release Your Expressive Powers

To unleash creativity in your writing (even if what you're trying to write is a college math book), you need to balance the right-brain linear mind with the left-brain mind where poetry, fantasy, daydreams, and all sorts of nonlinear thinking reside. This book provides exercises to access the right brain for creative development; these exercises stimulate imaginative thinking, so they may interest even those Witches who could care less about writing.

Bertrand Harris Bronson
The Singing Tradition of Child's Popular Ballads

If you want to sing English and Scottish ballads (folk songs that tell a story, often with mythical content), this is where you go. My friend Gwen, who is an accomplished balladeer, tells me this is the single best one-volume anthology of ballads available. More than 100 ballads are represented; for many of the ballads, multiple tunes and variations are presented in the text.

Julie Forest Middleton, editor and compiler
Songs for Earthlings: A Green Spirituality Songbook

Kate Marks, compiler
Circle of Song: Songs, Chants, and Dances for Ritual and Celebration

Two anthologies of songs and chants for ritual and ceremonial use. Largely, but not exclusively Pagan, both collections include plenty of songs appropriate for Wiccan use. *Songs for Earthlings* collects songs for the elements, the ancestors, the Wheel of the Year, and the cycles of life; *Circle of Song* includes numbers for creating sacred space, honoring all our relations, and both male and female power.

Layne Redmond
When the Drummers Were Women: A Spiritual History of Rhythm

Centuries before sensitive New Age guys went out in the woods to bang on their drums as an act of male solidarity, the drum—especially the frame drum—had a long and important history as an instrument of devotion to the Goddess. For women (and men) in our time, the drum can serve as a way to re-train our body-mind system to synchronize and connect on all levels of rhythm: the rhythm of the heart, the lungs, the Earth, the mother's womb, and of course, the drum. In Redmond's hands, drumming is elevated from mere entertainment to become a sacred tool for spiritual transformation. Sure, shamans have known that all along, but Redmond reminds us that drumming is not just a boy's club.

Rosina-Fawzia Al-Rawi
Grandmother's Secrets: The Ancient Rituals and Healing Power of Belly Dancing

Erotic and sensuous, belly dancing powerfully affirms feminine sexuality and—as this charming memoir by dance virtuoso Al-Rawi makes clear—functions as a ritualistic tool for healing and self-discovery. This story of a grandmother initiating the child into the mysteries of dance has an obvious parallel in the family traditions where a crone ushers her granddaughter into the ways of the Goddess.

Ruth St. Denis
Wisdom Comes Dancing: Selected Writings of Ruth St. Denis on Dance, Spirituality, and the Body

Lovely anthology of poems and essays by one of the mothers of modern dance, exploring the unity between sensuality and spirituality as manifest in the dancing body. Her spiritual vision is universalist in nature, and her poetry especially reflects a Goddess sensibility. Also includes photographs of the author performing.

Eleanor and Philip Harris
The Crafting and Use of Ritual Tools: Step-by-Step Instructions for Woodcrafting Religious and Magical Implements

Learn how to make a variety of ceremonial objects, including staffs, wands, runes, blade handles, and shields. This book also includes suggestions on consecrating tools for magical use.

Jim Hrisoulas
The Complete Bladesmith: Forging Your Way to Perfection

Perhaps most Witches will stick to herbcraft and blending oils, but for those who have an interest in hammering out their own athame, this book serves as a handy reference. Hrisoulas, himself a master bladesmith, provides instruction on setting up your own forge, selecting the materials, as well as step-by-step instructions on fashioning grips, hilts, and the blade itself.

Evan John Jones with Chas S. Clifton
Sacred Mask Sacred Dance

To wear a mask means to take on another persona; to dance means to engage in a choreographed movement with a meaning and story of its own. Ritual, shamanism, and magick all have employed masking and dancing as elements of spiritual practice. This book not only celebrates the place of the mask and the dance in Pagan spirituality, but also includes instructions on making your own ritual mask.

Charles Arnold
Ritual Body Art: Drawing the Spirit

Transform your body into a ritual implement, by painting magickal symbols onto it as part of enacting a ritual. The author explores how body adornment (not only painting the body, but jewelry, face makeup, and masking) can express powerful inner truths in a visually beautiful outer way. Includes a dictionary of symbols and color symbolism, and recipes for oils that can be used in body adornment.

George Leonard
Mastery: The Keys to Success and Long-Term Fulfillment

Part of the spiritual journey of creative development includes facing our inner obstacles and fears that hold us back from achieving excellence or mastery in our chosen artist outlet. George Leonard considers the pathway toward becoming a master athlete, and the principles he celebrates in this little book apply equally well to art, business, or even spirituality.

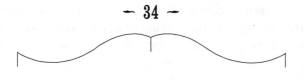

FICTION
FOR GROWNUPS

In the previous chapter, I pointed out that the ancient bards in the Celtic lands were the storytellers who preserved the memory of the people through the poems and legends. In telling their stories or singing their songs, the bards could weave a spell of enchantment over their audience. In our day, I believe storytelling and magick still have a profound connection. We first learn of the Goddess and the God through the ancient stories that are preserved in mythology. Magickal and mystical experiences become immortalized in stories, novels, folklore, and now even movies (think of the spiritual overtones in Dorothy's shamanic journey to the Fairy-land of Oz and in the hero's journey of Luke Skywalker, who masters the esoteric teachings of the Jedi Knights so that he might face the dark Lord Vader). Stories preserve the fundamental principles of shamanism, mysticism, and magick. This is why, when we've found ourselves fully immersed in a good movie or gripping book, we say it left us spellbound. What avid reader hasn't had the experience of delving into a particularly good novel, only to have time speed by while enraptured by the seemingly timeless experience of enjoying the story? A well-told story, whether true or fictional, has the power to enchant and enrapture those who hear or read it.

Most Wiccans understand that Nature can teach the ways of the Spirit far better than a book ever could. Even so, a well-told tale can help us find our way to the Goddess and the God; a good story can shimmer with magick, wonder, and a sense of mystical presence. Stories where characters encounter the numinous or spiritual world or where they master skills of magick to overcome conflict or challenge, can in turn inspire us to search for our own portal into the realm of wonders. And so, the books considered here range from historical fiction looking at life in ancient times (from Marion Zimmer Bradley's retelling of the Arthurian myth to Clysta Kinstler's imaginative depiction of Mari Magdalene as a Goddess devotee), to visionary speculations of the future (as in Robert Heinlein's or Ernest Callenbach's novels), to magickal excursions within the present day world (as in the writing of Tom Robbins or Margaret Atwood). Exploring these books can open us up to a magickal way of viewing the world, but perhaps more importantly, they're simply great stories that are fun to read.

Marion Zimmer Bradley
The Mists of Avalon

Classic retelling of the Arthurian saga, specifically from the perspective of Morgaine (Morgan Le Fay), who is depicted not in the usual way as an agent of darkness, but as a priestess of the Goddess who is watching her world crumble at the arrival of new customs and a new religion with a new god. A touching and sad book, but majestic and filled with reverence for the Mother.

Katherine Kurtz
Lammas Night

It's a footnote in Wiccan history that the Witches of England raised a cone of power in August 1940 to stop the impending German invasion of England—an invasion that, indeed, never happened. In *Lammas Night*, Katherine Kurtz weaves an enchanting story based on that Cone of Power, playfully weaving real characters (Gerald Gardner and Dion Fortune are among the historical figures who appear in this book) among the fictional Witches who comprise the main characters.

Clysta Kinstler
The Moon Under Her Feet

Wiccans who grew up in the Christian faith or who would like to reclaim their sense of Jesus as a magickal and powerful spiritual teacher will love this feminist retelling of the life of Christ. The narrator is Mari Magdalene, but Jesus' mother also figures prominently in this story. Both of these women are dedicants to the Great Mother Goddess, trying to maintain their Devotion to the Divine Feminine in a world where patriarchal religion is on the rise.

Starhawk
The Fifth Sacred Thing

Starhawk
Walking to Mercury

Before she became one of the most successful and respected of Wiccan authors (thanks to *The Spiral Dance*), Starhawk's ambition as a writer involved writing fiction. With these two books, she tells the story of Maya, a wise woman/healer of the future who lives in a world that encompasses two cultures— one based on spirituality, nonviolence, and harmony with Nature; the other an authoritarian, patriarchal police state. The

escalation of conflict between these opposing societies provides the grand backdrop for Starhawk's vision, one in which
progressive politics and Goddess spirituality unite in the
author's comprehensive vision of a possible utopia.

Ernest Callenbach
Ecotopia: A Novel

Hailed as an environmental classic, this story considers a
possible future where northern California, Oregon, and Wash-
ington state secede from the United States to establish an ecologically sustainable culture. Sexual politics, ritual, Nature
worship, and environmental politics combine in this glimpse
into what could happen if a culture makes ecology its highest
priority.

Robert A. Heinlein
Stranger in a Strange Land

This mid-20th-century novel might offend some because of
its embarrassingly pre-feminist language; some of the dialogue
certainly sounds sexist and patronizing. But Heinlein's vision
as presented here is hardly patriarchal. From its lampooning
of organized religion to its idealistic celebration of polyamorous
sex, many of the themes of this book are consistent with the
values of at least some segments of the Pagan community. The
book tells the story of a human being who was orphaned on
Mars, raised by aliens, only to return to earth to start a new
religion of devotion and free love called the Church of All
Worlds (and yes, there's a Pagan community of the same name
that was inspired by this book).

Reyna Thera Lorele
The Archer King: Robin of the Wood & the Maid Maerin

A retelling of the Robin Hood myth from a Wiccan/Druidic
perspective. Set against the background of England during the

crusades, this story deftly weaves the familiar elements of the lord of Sherwood Forest together with a consideration of the spiritual politics of old and new religion coexisting uneasily during a dangerous time.

Tom Robbins
Jitterbug Perfume

A trippy, olfactory excursion from present-day Seattle to medieval Europe, woven together by the secret of immortality—with fleas in Sweden, the nature of beets, and a janitor who can't find his bottle of perfume mixed in for good measure. Oh, yes, Pan has a part to play as well. My description may seem weird, but it's nothing compared to what you'll find when you actually read this funny, thoughtful, spiritual book.

Margaret Atwood
Surfacing

Dark and disturbing but ultimately redemptive, this story of a woman's shattering experience of reconnection/rebirth within the wilderness of the Canadian north explodes the tradition of macho writers like James Dickey and Ernest Hemingway, to create a deeply feminine encounter with the untamable country that lies not only at the edges of civilization, but deep within the soul.

Dion Fortune
The Sea Priestess

An occult novel featuring a Hermetic Initiate, Vivien Le Fay Morgan, who (as her name suggests) can transform herself into Morgan Le Fay, not only of Arthurian lore, but a priestess of Atlantis as well. In some ways this books shows its age, but the themes of Goddess spirituality and union with the gods as a means to the channeling of Nature's energy can still make for entertaining reading even today.

Naomi Mitchison
The Corn King and the Spring Queen

The story of an ancient Scythian sorceress's quest for redemption. Set in the third century B.C.E., this lyrical novel explores the culture and spirituality of the ancient Mediterranean world, where mysticism, ritual, and political intrigue form the backdrop of the heroine's quest. With a woman protagonist undergoing the hero's journey, this book (first published in 1931) was years ahead of its time.

Terry Pratchett
Wyrd Sisters

A playful and rollicking installment of Terry Pratchett's long-running Discworld series of fantasy novels. The (mis)adventures of three Witches, Granny Weatherwax, Nanny Ogg, and Magrat Garlick, whose lives as ordinary wisewomen are thrown into turmoil when a king is murdered, and his infant son winds up in their witchy care. A fun story set in a world where magick is no more unusual than anything else.

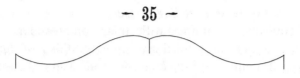

35

FICTION FOR KIDS

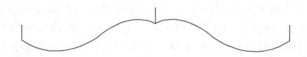

Pablo Picasso once said we should not teach the children to paint, but rather should let them teach the adults. His wisdom may apply just as much to spirituality and magick as it does to art. Kids have a natural affinity to magick; it hasn't been ironed out of them (yet) by the limiting thought-patterns they encounter in school and on television. Nowhere does the innate magick of childhood appear more readily than in stories and novels written for and about children. As a friend of mine who is an expert on children's literature pointed out, "If an adult novelist wants to include magick in his story, he has to take 30 or 40 pages to explain what he's going to do. But in a children's book, no such explanations are necessary. The magick happens, and the kids accept it."

Kids books are great fun, and I've really enjoyed doing the research necessary to write this chapter. From sinking my teeth into a current young adult bestseller (the Harry Potter series), to discovering some classics from a few years back (like Susan Cooper's *The Dark is Rising* sequence), my experience with these books has been filled with delight and wonder.

This chapter includes books for both younger and older children. For the little ones, a selection of illustrated books captures the mystery and excitement of life both through word and image. These include educationally oriented books like Susan Jeffers' *Brother Eagle, Sister Sky* and Becky McCarley's and Phil Travers' *Herman's Magical Universe*. But other titles simply tell a good story, although each of the books included here explores some sort of magickal or Nature-spirituality theme.

For the older kids, the selection of books profiled here explore both magick and mythology. In addition to magick and mysticism, these books explore topics as diverse as time travel (a 20th-century boy encounters the sixth-century Welsh bard Taliesin), ethical issues (Harry Potter and company learn right from wrong in their magickal studies) and environmental concerns (how destroying a stand of virgin forest has not only ecological, but spiritual repercussions). In each of these tales, the normal rules of life are bent, if not broken, and in the non-ordinary reality, the main characters of the stories become heroes in the mythic sense of the word, engaging in quests that lead to spiritual growth and transformation.

So children's literature revisits the hero's journey, a theme that has been explored in a scholarly way by the likes of Joseph Campbell. Children, being naturally more intelligent and intuitive than adults, generally don't have much use for scholarship or academic theories. They simply want to enjoy a good story. And so, in that spirit, here's a collection of good stories that any Wiccan—of any age—ought to love.

For younger kids...

Lynn Plourde and Greg Couch (illustrator)
Wild Child

A linguistically-playful story of Mother Earth trying to tuck her wild child (a little Nature Sprite) into bed. A poetic tale brimming with sensual imagery, accompanied by gorgeous illustrations, golden-hued glimpses into a Fairy-like realm where Mother Earth gently rises out of the landscape to lovingly caress her playful little imp. When the wild child finally yawns and teeters off to bed, Mother Earth's final comments (and what happens next) will bring a smile to anyone who feels love and wonder at the turning of the seasons.

Douglas Wood and Cheng-Khee Chee (illustrator)
Old Turtle

A touching fable in which all the animals and the elements of Nature have an argument about what God is like. Then the old turtle, who "hardly ever said anything and certainly never argued about God" gave the animals insight into the true nature of the Divine, as well as a warning for the youngest and most forgetful animal of all—the human. This award-winning bestseller is an example of how a truly Nature-oriented spirituality is slowly creeping into the mainstream of society. The illustrations are charming, and the story will touch the heart of anyone who understands the fundamental unity between God (or Goddess) and Nature.

Douglas Wood and P. J. Lynch (illustrator)
Grandad's Prayers of the Earth

The author of *Old Turtle* returns with a gentle tale of his childhood—about how his grandfather taught him to pray. God never gets mentioned in this book, but Nature is all over it. "Like the trees and winds and waters, we pray because we are here—not to change the world, but to change ourselves.

Because it is when we change ourselves...that the world is changed," says Grandad. Another mainstream book with a positive message concerning Nature spirituality.

Debra Frasier
On the Day You Were Born
A song of benediction and love for a newborn child, in which the earth, the sun, the moon, and the stars join together with all the creatures of the earth in welcoming the baby into the world. A simple story about the beauty of Nature and how all things are interconnected.

Susan Jeffers (illustrator)
Brother Eagle, Sister Sky: A message from Chief Seattle
An environmentalist message for kids of all ages. "The earth does not belong to us. We belong to the earth." These powerful words attributed to Chief Seattle, who warned white Americans to live in harmony with Nature. Beautiful imagery of the web of life provides the background against which Seattle challenges his conquerors to treat the environment with reverence and respect.

Becky McCarley and Phil Travers (illustrator)
Herman's Magical Universe
The story of a 7-year-old who seeks, and learns, the basic principles of Hermetic philosophy. Through discovering seven laws of the universe, Herman embarks on the lifelong journey to become an alchemical master.

Clare Walker Leslie and Frank E. Gerace
The Ancient Celtic Festivals: And How We Celebrate Them Today
Okay, so this isn't fiction. But it's a wonderful little book, perfect for budding Pagans. Who were the Celts, and how

have their Nature-based holidays survived into modern times? This book connects the dots between Imbolc and Groundhog's Day and between Samhain and Halloween. Wiccan parents can use this as a starting point to discuss differences between Pagans and non-Pagans in our society.

For older kids...

J. K. Rowling
Harry Potter And The Sorcerer's Stone

J. K. Rowling
Harry Potter and the Chamber of Secrets

J. K. Rowling
Harry Potter and the Prisoner of Azkaban

J. K. Rowling
Harry Potter and the Goblet of Fire

Some Wiccans don't like the Harry Potter books, because they don't always get the details of Witchcraft right. Filled with toads and goblins and icky-tasting jellybeans, these stories revel in oogie-boogie stereotypes of Witchery. But it's all in good fun, and Harry Potter's adventures not only present magickal spirituality in a favorable light, but more importantly, affirm an ethical approach to the Occult. A bonus: with the religious right so up in arms about these books, an entire generation of young people is learning that censorship is bogus. Three more volumes are planned for the future.

Susan Cooper
The Dark is Rising Sequence
(Over Sea, Under Stone; The Dark is Rising; Greenwitch; The Grey King; Silver on the Tree)

The story of Will Stanton and the Drew children, and their adventures engaging in the eternal struggle between the light and the dark, as it plays out on the mythic landscape of Welsh (especially Arthurian) tradition. Filled with Arthurian and Welsh Pagan mythology, these books explore archetypal magick with a mature look at the eternal conflict of good and evil.

Nancy Bond
A String in the Harp

A tale of magickal time travel, as 20th-century kids enter into the world of the sixth century Welsh bard, Taliesin. An American boy, unhappy at having to spend a year living in rural Wales, discovers a mystical doorway into the heritage of the Pagan past. The messy dynamics of a modern dysfunctional family provide the backdrop for an introduction to the world of the Welsh epic *Mabinogion*.

T. A. Barron
The Ancient One

When Kate goes on vacation to visit her Aunt Melanie in the Pacific Northwest, they stumble on a remote stand of virgin forest that loggers want to harvest—but that holds a secret portal to the past, where Kate encounters the Halami, a tribe of Native Americans. Along with being a great story, this book makes a strong statement for preserving both the natural world and the cultural heritage of indigenous people.

Diana Wynne Jones
Charmed Life

Diana Wynne Jones
The Lives of Christopher Chant

Diana Wynne Jones
The Magicians of Caprona

Diana Wynne Jones
Witch Week

Set in a Harry Potter-like world brimming with magick and Witches and spells, these novels follow the adventures of two orphans, Cat and Gwendolyn, who go to live with Mrs. Sharp on Coven Street. There, Gwendolyn undergoes training as a Witch, but Cat seems to be a boy with no magickal ability. Whimsical, and at times, hilarious tales of shadow universes, ethical magick, and plenty of "oogie-boogie" to keep the kids smiling.

Nancy Springer
The Hex Witch of Seldom

A story with powerful archetypal overtones. Set in Pennsylvania Dutch Country, this coming of age story concerns a psychically gifted teenage girl who loves a mustang horse, which represents the archetype of the noble outlaw. Greater than a man and less than a god, the archetypal outlaw has been imprisoned in the figure of the horse. The story follows the girl's efforts to help the horse regain his authentic self; in doing so, she discovers her own true identity.

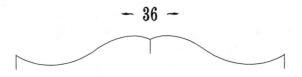

36

REFERENCE BOOKS

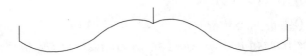

Every magickal library needs its share of reference works: dictionaries, encyclopedias, and other collections of helpful data. Although such books rarely make for interesting cover-to-cover reading, they nonetheless provide useful information in a handy, easy-to-find format. Many of the books that I've profiled have reference sections (see *The Spiral Dance* in Chapter 6 for an excellent example of a beginner's book with a useful reference section), but the books profiled in this chapter are reference tools through and through.

Whether providing lists of magickal correspondences, background information on critical issues (such as the relationship between Witchcraft and law enforcement), or questions of Pagan protocol and etiquette, each of these titles provides handy knowledge for the day-to-day life of a Witch.

This chapter also includes a selection of books on Pagan parenting. When interest in Wicca first exploded in the 1960s and 70s, it appealed primarily to the young generation. Years have gone by, and today Wiccans come in all shapes, sizes, and ages. This means more and more followers of the old ways have families, and face questions of religious education; explaining the difference between Pagan spirituality and other religions; and how to teach a child about things like magick, sexuality, and environmentalism, where Pagan values often differ from the values of mainstream society. As more and more Pagans have faced parenting issues, wonderful books have come along to address their concerns.

General reference

Lady Galadriel, editor
A New Wiccan Book of the Law: A Manual for the Guidance of Groves, Covens, and Individuals, Second edition

While Wicca has a single ethical mandate in the Wiccan rede, most traditions acknowledge a set of laws that govern the customs, practices, and smooth administration of covens within the old religion. Different versions of Wiccan law exist, as taught by various Craft traditions. By the mid-1980s, Lady Galadriel of the Unicorn Tradition had several such versions in her possession. In her words, "I decided to do something daring—I took the four different versions of the Laws which I had, and combined and reworked them. I deleted what was no longer pertinent and meaningful, rewording others to make them clearer and more understandable, as well as adding some new ones which I felt had been lacking." Kudos to her for her honesty about this delicate balancing act between preserving tradition and contributing to its ongoing evolution. Today, a variety of traditions use Lady Galadriel's version of the Wiccan law. Of course, no one set of Laws could be deemed the standard in a tradition so organically decentralized as Wicca, but *A New Wiccan Book of the Law* comes as close as anything to presenting Wiccan law in a comprehensive and universal way.

Rosemary Ellen Guiley
The Encyclopedia of Witches and Witchcraft, Revised edition

A useful compendium of data on Witchcraft both past and present. With more than 400 entries, this book (unlike some other Witchcraft encyclopedias on the market) approaches the topic from a positive Wiccan perspective, rather than from a sensationalist Witchcraft-as-black-magick stance.

Selena Fox et. al, editors
Circle Guide to Pagan Groups: A Nature Spirituality Networking Sourcebook

Young Wiccans may barely remember a time before the World Wide Web served as the tool Witches used to find one another; but once upon a time, old-timer Pagans had to rely on networking organizations like Circle Sanctuary to help us connect. Even with all the Internet has to offer, this guidebook is still a valuable resource, if for no other reason than it provides information on various groups, stores, and gatherings in an easy-to-read and easy-to-use format. It's hardly exhaustive, but it can help both beginners and veterans to stay connected.

June G. Bletzer, Ph.D.
The Encyclopedic Psychic Dictionary

Here's a comprehensive dictionary/encyclopedia of psychic, spiritualist, and metaphysical terms and concepts. Although geared more toward old-school mediumship and related spiritualist practices, the book is up-to-date enough to include sympathetic entries on Wicca and Neopagan Witches, and a mostly-positive entry on Witches. With over 9000 entries covering over 800 pages, this reference is jammed full of information. Anyone who is conducting research into the psychic sciences will find this utterly invaluable.

Rex E. Bills
The Rulership Book: A Directory of Astrological Correspondences

Although written for astrologers, the information contained in this book can benefit any magician. Every aspect of life is ruled by one or more of the elements of astrology—the planets, the houses, and the zodiac signs. This book, which is almost like a magickal thesaurus, categorizes what each of the planets, signs, and houses rules: for example, money is ruled by Venus, sexuality is ruled by Pluto, and Witchcraft is ruled by Neptune. This in-depth list of correspondences can assist in scheduling (and designing) rituals and spells in harmony with events in the sky.

Barbara G. Walker
The Woman's Encyclopedia of Myths and Secrets

Barbara G. Walker
The Woman's Dictionary of Symbols and Sacred Objects

Two exhaustive collections of cultural information, particularly relevant to women's spiritual power, both in history and for today. Myths of the Goddess in her many guises, secrets of fairy tales, folklore, and religious rites, along with numerous images, symbols, customs, and key figures in the feminine/feminist tradition. With literally thousands of entries between these books on an array of magickal and wondrous topics, these resources provide valuable information to anyone working to reclaim the long-suppressed feminine dimension of spirituality for our time.

Scott Cunningham
Cunningham's Encyclopedia of Magical Herbs

Scott Cunningham
Cunningham's Encyclopedia of Crystal, Gem, & Metal Magic

Two popular compendiums of magickal lore and psychic speculation on herbal and mineral correspondences. Helpful as guidelines for developing your own mystical relationship with plants and minerals.

Rosemary Ellen Guiley
Harper's Encyclopedia of Mystical & Paranormal Experience

A collection of esoteric information from around the globe. Includes useful overviews of Eastern and Western spirituality, speculative science, psychic and metaphysical lore, and various aspects of Occultism. This is a balanced and general overview of the frontiers of spiritual experience.

Leonard George, Ph.D.
Alternative Realities: The Paranormal, the Mystic, and the Transcendent in Human Experience

Approximately 450 in-depth entries on an array of weird and unusual goings-on, from altered states of consciousness to zazen, from the abominable snowman to zombification. The author attempts to present his non-ordinary subject matter in a critical but balanced way.

Kerr Cuhulain
The Law Enforcement Guide To Wicca

Excellent overview of Pagan religions, written by a police officer and the author of *Wiccan Warrior* (Chapter 12). If you are doing any kind of Pagan public outreach, or have any dealings with law enforcement, this book provides a clear delineation of what Nature spirituality entails. Especially useful for quelling anxieties about Satanism that have been promoted by overzealous fundamentalists.

Parenting

Starhawk, Diane Baker, and Anne Hil
Circle Round: Raising Children in Goddess Traditions

A beautifully illustrated guide to kid-friendly rituals, celebrations, and Goddess-oriented stories. Includes activities, crafts, and rituals for the Wheel of the Year, the Elements, and the life cycle. I've known more than one priestess who has incorporated ideas from this book into rituals for adults—that's how good they are.

Ashleen O'Gaea
The Family Wicca Book: The Craft for Parents and Children

Kristin Madden
Pagan Parenting: Spiritual, Magical & Emotional Development of the Child

Ceisiwr Serith
The Pagan Family: Handing the Old Ways Down

Evidence that the Pagan/Wiccan community is maturing may be found in these three books written for parents raising children in the Old Ways. Combining information on the Pagan worldview with ritual ideas and good old fashioned parenting tips, these books can be a helpful friend to the parent faced with the challenging task of raising a child in accordance with the values of a minority religion—a situation where finding practical support may sometimes be difficult.

37

THE WELL-WIRED WITCH

Once upon a time (a long, long time ago, say before 1993), almost nobody had access to the Internet. Back then, Wiccans had to rely on books, magickal and occult stores, and a few national networking organizations (like Covenant of the Goddess or Circle Sanctuary) to find others interested in the Craft. Nowadays, all it takes is a modem and the courage to enter the word "Witch" into your favorite search engine.

Pagan and Wiccan spirituality has achieved an impressive online presence. This is really not that surprising, for the Wiccan community, like the Lesbian/Gay community or other alternative groups, often faces discrimination or harsh criticism in the real world but can present itself favorably in the anonymous slipstreams of cyberspace. Plus, with the exception of a handful of big money Web sites such as Amazon or Ebay, much of the real estate online has remained in the hands of individuals who create Web sites for love, rather than for profit. The Internet and Wicca are both refuges for those who think our multi-conglomerated world has become just a little too centralized, a little too profit-driven, a little too standardized. Alternative thinkers can find a home both in cyberspace and in the old religion.

So will the Internet eventually replace books? Will online grimoires and teaching curricula render classics like *The Spiral Dance* obsolete? I personally don't think so. Just as television didn't destroy the book, neither will cyberspace. Sure, there may be new ways in which the content of books are delivered (like e-books or other electronic tools), but the book itself—the complex, in-depth text—will continue to have a place in our culture, as long as there are curious, intelligent seekers (not only in Wicca, but in any area of human inquiry). The Internet, with its colorful graphics and bite-sized Web pages, represents a new style or form of communication, that ultimately will complement and enhance books, not replace them. Indeed, more than a few of the Web sites listed here have recommended reading lists, pointing to how Web developers—and surfers—tend also to be voracious readers.

This roundup of Wiccan and Wiccan-friendly Web sites includes a few of the best known Pagan sites like Witchvox or Isaac Bonewits' home page, that have become magnets for magickally-oriented Web surfers. But I've included a few lesser-known URLs as well, covering topics as diverse as Gardnerian Wicca, world mythology, and religious tolerance. None of these sites operate on fat ad budgets or Wall Street capital; rather, the sites listed here are homegrown, amateur operations that nevertheless exhibit a high degree of design sophistication and quality content (okay, so not all these sites are well designed. But I think it's wonderful to get off the beaten path of the Internet and find Web sites that weren't developed by professional Web designers, but still contain oodles of useful information).

With just one visit to the Witches' Voice or to a Pagan-friendly search engine like AvatarSearch (*www.avatarsearch.com*) or

Ariadne Spider (*www.ariadnespider.com*), you'll have access to an onslaught of Wiccan Web sites—of varying quality. Everything I mentioned in Chapter 3 on how to identify the best books applies equally well to the search for the best Web sites.

The Witches' Voice
www.witchvox.com

Probably the largest and most useful Wiccan Web site, Witches' Voice (or WitchVox) offers news related to Paganism updated daily, along with thousands of links to Pagan groups, authors, merchants, and other Web sites. The site also includes networking information on groups without Web sites. Their home page states, "WitchVox doesn't teach Witchcraft, give out spells or accept paid advertising. We are a non-commercial, community driven resource."

Circle Sanctuary
www.circlesanctuary.org

Founded in 1974 by Selena Fox, Circle Sanctuary sponsors gatherings and encourages Nature preservation through its spiritual and networking efforts. Circle advocates religious freedom through the Lady Liberty League and fosters interfaith dialogue to improve cooperation and exchange between religious bodies. Circle Network, an information exchange and contact service, links together both individuals and organizations of Nature spirituality practitioners throughout the world.

Covenant of the Goddess
www.cog.org

COG, founded in 1975, is an international organization of cooperating, autonomous Wiccan congregations and solitary practitioners. It provides information to the media and others on the Craft, and supports its members by providing legal credentials for Wiccan clergy. While there's not much on the Web site for non-members, several articles, links, and information for youth make this site worth a visit.

The Pagan Federation
www.paganfed.demon.co.uk

This UK-based group plays a role similar to COG or Circle in North America, as a networking and educational umbrella organization. Although the Pagan Federation does not as of this writing have much of a presence in the United States, it is an international organization with contacts in Sweden, Belgium, the Netherlands, Canada, Germany, Austria, and Switzerland, as well as the UK.

Isaac Bonewits' Home Page
www.neopagan.net

The author of *Real Magic* is an opinionated sort who has fashioned a comprehensive Web site full of articles, essays, rants, and reviews. Also check out the Ár nDraíocht Féin Web site (*www.adf.org*). Founded by Bonewits, ADF is probably the largest Pagan Druid organization active today, with an emphasis on scholarship and academic excellence without sacrificing the magickal/shamanic dimension of primal Euroshamanism.

The Third Road
www.well.com/~zthirdrd

and

The Grove of the Unicorn
www.unicorntrad.com

Home pages of the Witches I interviewed in Chapter 2: Francesca De Grandis and Lady Galadriel. Each of these Web sites offers an abundance of material on Craft lore, along with background information on the traditions they represent. The Unicorn Web site also has ordering information for Lady Galadriel's books, all of which are self-published and not widely available.

Beaufort House
www.geocities.com/SoHo/5756

The Beaufort House Association is an ad-hoc working group of Elders from various lineages of English Traditional Witchcraft. This no-frills Web site ("without animated pentacles and flickering flames") includes information on Gardnerian and other traditions of British Witchcraft. Two highlights include a family tree index of traditional lineages, and "The Witch's Duty of Care," an essay about the responsibilities of the Witch.

Gardnerian Agora
www.gardnerian.net

Another no-frills site. Information and links specifically on the Gardnerian lineage. These days, most Gardnerians shy away from publicity, so this site has little in the way of contacts or networking links, but instead provides just enough information to tantalize the seeker who wants to find a traditional coven.

Resources for Coven Leaders
www.usit.com/tnglmoon/covenleaders.htm

A collection of useful articles and information for coven and other group leaders. Although it's a more fancily designed site than the Gardnerian or Beaufort House sites, it is still a homegrown site given freely to the Internet community by the Tangled Moon Coven of Tennessee. Some of the topics covered here include the role of excellence in group leadership, finding and screening potential new students, counseling basics, and a checklist for a well-working group. Additional links as well as a few recommended books round out this resource.

Ontario Consultants on Religious Tolerance
www.religioustolerance.org

Wiccans know too well how freedom of religion often does not extend to the practitioners of minority faiths. For this reason, we need to support this excellent, award-winning Web site dedicated to fostering religious tolerance as a basic civil right. It is objective in its coverage of the old religion and includes an interesting page on efforts to estimate the number of Pagan and Wiccan practitioners in North America.

Encyclopedia Mythica
www.pantheon.org

Online since 1995, this gorgeously designed Web site consists of an encyclopedia covering mythology, folklore, heroes, and legends, containing more than 5,000 definitions of Gods and Goddesses, supernatural beings, and legendary creatures from all over the world. The site has a search function; a good thing, too, for the database contains over 200 articles each on Celtic and Egyptian mythology, and over 600 entries on Greek mythology.

The Well-Read Witch
www.wellreadwitch.com

And finally, the Web site for this book. While conducting my research for this project, this Web site featured several surveys so Web surfers could recommend books they had found useful (thanks to everyone who participated). For the future, the Web site will include new reviews and recommendations, basically for books published (or that come to my attention) after this book goes to press. So to stay updated on what's exciting in the world of Wiccan literature (and to keep your must-read list growing indefinitely), stop by for a visit.

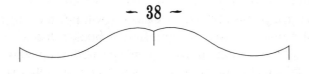

HOW TO FIND BOOKS
(ESPECIALLY WHEN
THEY'RE OUT OF PRINT)

I've had tremendous fun putting together this list of books. I hope you've enjoyed reading through it as much as I've enjoyed drawing it up. Now, one key question remains: where do you go to purchase these books?

Many of the books listed here are, unfortunately, out of print. Others are in print and pretty much available at any bookstore. Still others are published by relatively small or obscure companies, and therefore only available through bookstores that specialize in metaphysical or occult subjects. Unfortunately, with the publishing business being increasingly dominated by a few megaconglomerate corporations that care more about the bottom line than about the importance of literature, more and more of the books profiled here may go out of print with each passing year—after all, as of this writing, Wicca is still not exactly bestseller material, and some publishers seem to think that only bestsellers deserve to get published—or stay in print. On the other hand, new technologies (such as e-books or print-on-demand books) may make it easier to find more obscure titles, since publishers and booksellers will not have to invest lots of money to stock many different books; instead, books will be stored on computers and only printed when consumers request them. This means that valuable (but slow selling) books, like many of the ones reviewed here, will be available once again. As of this writing (summer 2001) e-books and print-on-demand are technologies still in their infancy, but I predict in years to come, more and more books will be available through these electronic means of distribution.

Back to the question of where to buy books. I'd like to encourage my readers to support, as much as possible, your neighborhood, locally-owned-and-operated metaphysical or occult bookstore. These are the stores that stocked books on Witchcraft, Goddess spirituality, and natural magick long before such topics became trendy or faddish. Which means they will continue to support our spiritual path even if it stops being trendy. The local metaphysical stores are almost always operated by people with a passion for mysticism and spirituality, and a healthy respect for minority paths such as ours. Indeed, at most metaphysical stores you will find knowledgeable clerks who can help you with recommendations and reviews of what's new and what's hot. Also, locally owned bookstores can usually fill special orders faster than the big chain bookstores, and can even order books from tiny little independent publishers. That's because independent retailers don't have to wade through mounds of red tape to place a special order or to get a book from an obscure source. Of course, sometimes a book might be more readily available online or through a big chain store, but at least try to get it through the independent store first.

The quest for the holy grail

But what about when a book is not available at all from the publisher? Out of print books pose a difficult problem for the book-loving Witch. Finding a no-longer-published book sometimes seems only slightly easier than tracking down the holy grail. Every major city has one or more used bookshops, and often these stores will have extensive holdings in occult or metaphysical titles. But it's always a roll of the dice whether or not the one book you're looking for might be in stock at such establishments. Then there are the Web sites run by the major conglomerate bookstores that offer to find out of print books for you. But often, when these Web sites do locate a book for you, it's horrendously overpriced.

So beware of shopping for used or out of print books online, with one exception: the Advanced Book Exchange, or *www.abebooks.com*. I heartily endorse this Web site because, instead of being a mega-corporate venture, it actually is a consortium of many small, independent, locally owned-and-operated bookstores. Each bookstore pays a small monthly fee to A.B.E. to list their inventory in the abebooks.com database. You, the consumer, can search the database for the books you want, and the Web site simply refers you to the independent bookstore that has your desired book in stock. You then deal directly with the bookseller. It's a great service; I think my wife rues the day I discovered abebooks.com, because I've spent quite a few dollars there, including buying many of the out of print titles that I've reviewed in this book! But don't let online booksellers distract you from looking for out of print books at brick-and-mortar stores. Even if you like to shop online, I still recommend finding one or two local bookstores in your community who specialize in used and out of print books. Get to know the owners and managers of such stores. Often times, such establishments will maintain a want list of books you are looking for, and if they find through their network a copy of a book on your list, they'll call you with the price. It's a great service that most used bookstores offer for free.

Here's another idea. Don't be shy about checking with the elders in your coven to see if they have copies of the books profiled here. Many of them do, and would be happy to lend you a book or two (provided you take scrupulously good care of them—remember, out of print books are not easily re-placed). I remember when I first purchased my copy of the long out of print (and expensive) *Moon, Moon* by Anne Kent Rush (profiled in Chapter 21). I showed it to a Wiccan elder. She smiled and reminisced, "back when I was first studying Witchcraft in the 1970s, that book was required reading in my coven. And now," she continued wistfully, "it's out of print." Hard to find, perhaps, but elders like her have copies of such rare books, and are usually willing to loan books to their dedicated (and responsible) students.

Remember: Today's out of print books were often yesterday's must-reads. Rely on your elders not only for the wisdom in their brains, take advantage of the wisdom on their bookshelves as well.

One last thought: If there's a book you wish to read and you can't find a copy anywhere, write to the publisher and ask them to either reprint it or at least to make it available online as an e-book or print-on-demand book. Of course, this strategy might take some time, but if everyone who wanted a book took the time to let the publisher know about it, many books might come back from being out of print.

Well, we've come to the end of this little book. But Wicca is a cyclical path, where every ending is also a beginning. Put this book down and start enjoying the books profiled in here; they'll add pleasure and knowledge to your journey into the mysteries of the Craft. Also remember, the wisdom of the Goddess is not found primarily in books, but rather deep in the whispers of the wind and the sea and the forest, and most especially in the whispers of your own heart. To the extent that books can help attune you to her whispering wisdom, then they have served their purpose. Read all the good books you can—and also remember to put the books down frequently and listen for the whisper of the Goddess and her beloved consort.

Blessed be!

Complete List of Books by Author

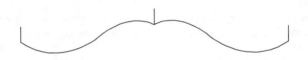

A

Abram, David. *The Spell of the Sensuous: Perception and Language in a More-Than-Human World*. Pantheon Books, 1996.

Achterberg, Jeanne, Ph.D., Barbara Dossey, R.N., M.S., FAAN, and Leslie Kolkmeier, R.N., M.Ed. *Rituals of Healing: Using Imagery for Health and Wellness*. Bantam Books, 1994.

Adams, Carol J. *Ecofeminism and the Sacred*. Continuum, 1993.

Adams, Cass, editor. *The Soul Unearthed: Celebrating Wildness and Personal Renewal Through Nature*. Tarcher/Putnam, 1996.

Adler, Margot. *Drawing Down the Moon: Witches, Druids, Goddess-Worshippers, and Other Pagans in America Today,* Revised and Expanded Edition. Penguin/Arkana, 1997.

Al-Rawi, Rosina-Fawzia. *Grandmother's Secrets: The Ancient Rituals and Healing Power of Belly Dancing*. Interlink Books, 1999.

Allrich, Karri. *Recipes from a Vegetarian Goddess: Delectable Feasts Through the Seasons*. Llewellyn Publications, 2000.

————. *A Witch's Book of Dreams: Understanding the Power of Dreams & Symbols*. Llewellyn Publications, 2001.

Altman, Nathaniel. *The Deva Handbook: How to Work with Nature's Subtle Energies*. Inner Traditions International, 1995.

Anand, Margo. *The Art of Sexual Ecstasy: The Path of Sacred Sexuality for Western Lovers*. Jeremy P. Tarcher/Putnam, 1989.

Anapol, Deborah, Ph.D., *Polyamory, The New Love Without Limits: Secrets of Sustainable Intimate Relationships*. IntiNet Resource Center, 1997.

Anderson, William. *Green Man: The Archetype of Our Oneness With the Earth*. Harper Collins, 1990.

Andrews, Ted. *Animal-Speak: The Spiritual & Magical Powers of Creatures Great & Small*. Llewellyn Publications, 1993.

———. *How to Meet and Work with Spirit Guides*. Llewellyn Publications, 1992.

———. *How to See and Read the Aura*. Llewellyn Publications, 1991

Ankarloo, Bengt, and Stuart Clark, editors. *Witchcraft and Magic in Europe* (six volume series). University of Pennsylvania Press, 1999-2001.

Apuleis (translated by Robert Graves). *The Transformations of Lucius Otherwise Known as The Golden Ass*. Farrar, Straus and Giroux, 1951.

Ardinger, Barbara, Ph.D. *Goddess Meditations*. Llewellyn Publications, 1998.

Arnold, Charles. *Ritual Body Art: Drawing the Spirit*. Phoenix Publishing, 1996.

Asala, Joanne. *Celtic Folklore Cooking*. Llewellyn Publications, 1998.

Ashcroft-Nowicki, Dolores. *Highways of the Mind: The Art and History of Pathworking*. Aquarian, 1987.

Aswynn, Freya. *Northern Mysteries and Magick: Runes, Gods, and Feminine Powers*. Llewellyn Publications, 1998.

Atwood, Margaret. *Surfacing*. Simon & Schuster, 1972.

Aveni, Anthony. *Behind the Crystal Ball: Magic, Science, and the Occult From Antiquity Through the New Age*. Times Books, 1996.

B

Baldwin, Christina. *Calling the Circle: The First and Future Culture*. Swan•Raven & Company, 1994.

Bardon, Franz. *Initiation into Hermetics: The Path of the True Adept*. Merkur Publishing, Inc., 1999.

Barrett, Clive. *The Egyptian Gods and Goddesses*. Aquarian/HarperCollins, 1991.

Barrett, Francis. *The Magus: A Complete System of Occult Philosophy*. Samuel Weiser, Inc., 2000 (originally published in 1801).

Barron, T.A. *The Ancient One*. Philomel Books, 1992.

Baynes, Cary F., translator. *The Richard Wilhelm Translation of the I Ching, or Book of Changes*. Princeton University Press, 1950.

Beck, Renee, and Sydney Barbara Metrick. *The Art of Ritual: A Guide to Creating and Performing Your Own Ceremonies for Growth and Change*. Celestial Arts, 1990.

Bentov, Itzhak. *Stalking the Wild Pendulum: On the Mechanics of Consciousness*. Destiny Books, 1977.

Berger, Helen A. *A Community of Witches: Contemporary Neo-Paganism and Witchcraft in the United States*. University of South Carolina Press, 1999.

Berger, Judith. *Herbal Rituals*. St. Martin's Griffin, 1998.

Berney, Charlotte. *Fundamentals of Hawaiian Mysticism*. Crossing Press, 2000.

Beyerl, Paul. *A Compendium of Herbal Magick*. Phoenix Publishing, 1998.

⸻. *The Master Book of Herbalism*. Phoenix Publishing, 1984.

⸻. *A Wiccan Bardo, Revisited: Initiation and Self-Transformation*. The Hermit's Grove, 1999.

Bills, Rex E. *The Rulership Book: A Directory of Astrological Correspondences*. American Federation of Astrologers, 1993.

Birrell, Anne M. *Chinese Mythology: An Introduction*. Johns Hopkins University Press, 1999.

Blacksun, *The Spell of Making*. Eschaton Productions, Inc., 1995.

Blanton, Brad, Ph.D. *Radical Honesty: How to Transform Your Life By Telling the Truth*. Dell Publishing, 1994.

Bletzer, June G., Ph.D. *The Encyclopedic Psychic Dictionary*. New Leaf Distributing Company, 1986.

Bolen, Jean Shinoda, M.D. *Gods in Every Man: A New Psychology of Men's Lives and Loves*. Harper Collins, 1989.

Bond, Nancy. *A String in the Harp*. Atheneum, 1976.

Bonewits, Isaac. *Real Magic: An Introductory Treatise on the Basic Principles of Yellow Magic*. Revised Edition, Samuel Weiser, 1989.

Bord, Janet and Colin. *Earth Rites: Fertility Practices in Pre-Industrial Britain*. Granada Publishing, Limited, 1982.

Boston Women's Health Book Collective. *Our Bodies, Ourselves for the New Century: A Book by and For Women*. Touchstone/Simon & Schuster, 1998.

Bown, Deni. *The Herb Society of America Encyclopedia of Herbs and Their Uses*. Dorling Kindersley, 1995.

Bradley, Marion Zimmer. *The Mists of Avalon*. Alfred A. Knopf, Inc., 1982.

Brennan,Barbara Ann. *Hands of Light: A Guide to Healing Through the Human Energy Field*. Bantam Books, 1987.

Brenneman, Walter L. Jr., and Mary G. *Crossing the Circle at the Holy Wells of Ireland*. University Press of Virginia, 1995.

Broch, Janice, and Veronica MacLer. *Seasonal Dance: How to Celebrate the Pagan Year*. Samuel Weiser, Inc., 1993.

Bronson, Bertrand Harris. *The Singing Tradition of Child's Popular Ballads*. Princeton Paperbacks, 1976.

Brown, Joseph Epes. *The Sacred Pipe: Black Elk's Account of the Seven Rites of the Oglala Sioux*. University of Oklahoma Press, 1953.

Buckland, Raymond. *Ancient and Modern Witchcraft: the Truth About Witchcraft By A Witch High Priest*. Castle Books, 1970.

_____. *Buckland's Complete Book of Witchcraft*. Llewellyn Publications, 1986.

_____. *Witchcraft From the Inside: Origins of the Fastest Growing Religious Movement in America*. Llewellyn Publications, 1971.

Budapest, Zsuzsanna. *The Holy Book of Women's Mysteries: Feminist Witchcraft, Goddess Rituals, Spellcasting, & Other Womanly Arts*. Wingbow Press, 1980.

Budilovsky, Joan, and Eve Adamson. *The Complete Idiot's Guide to Meditation*. Alpha Books, 1998.

Burkert, Walter. *Ancient Mystery Cults*. Harvard University Press, 1987.

_____.*Greek Religion*. Harvard University Press, 1985.

Butler, W. E. *How to Read the Aura and Practice Psychometry, Telepathy, and Clairvoyance*. Destiny Books, 1978.

C

Callenbach, Ernest. *Ecotopia: A Novel*. Bantam Books, 1975.

Cameron, Julia. *The Artist's Way: A Spiritual Path to Higher Creativity*. Tarcher/Putnam, 1992.

Campanelli, Pauline and Dan. *Pagan Rites of Passage*. Llewellyn Publications, 1994.

_____. *Wheel of the Year: Living the Magical Life*. Llewellyn Publications, 1989.

Campbell, Joseph. *The Hero With a Thousand Faces*. Princeton University Press, 1949.

Camphausen, Rufus C. *The Encyclopedia of Sacred Sexuality: From Aphrodisiacs and Ecstasy to Yoni Worship and Zap-lam Yoga*. Inner Traditions International, 1999.

Capra, Fritjof. *The Tao of Physics*. Third edition, updated, Shambhala Publications, Inc., 1991.

————.*The Turning Point: Science, Society, and the Rising Culture*. Simon & Schuster, 1982.

Carmichael, Alexander. *Carmina Gadelica: Hymns & Incantations Collected in the Highlands and Islands of Scotland in the Last Century*. Lindisfarne Press, 1992.

Carr-Gomm, Philip, editor. *The Druid Renaissance: the Voice of Druidry Today*. Thorsons, 1996.

————.*The Druid Way*. Element Books, Inc., 1993.

Carroll, David, and Barry Saxe. *Natural Magic: The Magical State of Being*. Arbor House, 1977.

Casey, Caroline W. *Making the Gods Work for You: the Astrological Language of the Psyche*. Harmony Books, 1998.

Cayce, Edgar. *Auras: An Essay on the Meaning of Colors*. A.R.E. Press, 1945.

Christ, Carol P. *Laughter of Aphrodite: Reflections on a Journey to the Goddess*. Harper Collins, 1987.

Cooper, Susan. *The Dark is Rising Sequence (Over Sea, Under Stone; The Dark is Rising; Greenwitch; The Grey King; Silver on the Tree)*. Guild America Books, 1965-1977.

Cope, Julian. *The Modern Antiquarian: A Pre-Millennial Odyssey Through Megalithic Britain*. Thorsons, 1998.

Cowan, Tom. *Fire in the Head: Shamanism and the Celtic Spirit*. Harper San Francisco, 1993.

————.*Shamanism as a Spiritual Practice for Daily Life*. Crossing Press, 1996.

Croft, Jack, editor. *The Doctors' Book of Home Remedies for Men, From Heart Disease and Headaches to Flabby Abs and Fatigue*. Men's Health Books, 1999.

Cross, Tom P., and Clark Harris Slover, editors. *Ancient Irish Tales*. Henry Holt & Company, 1936.

Crowley, Vivianne. *Phoenix from the Flame: Pagan Spirituality in the Western World*. Thorsons, 1994.

Crowley, Vivianne. *Wicca: The Old Religion in the New Millennium*. Thorsons, 1996.

Crowther, Patricia. *Lid Off the Cauldron: A Wicca Handbook*. Capall Bann Publishing, 1981.

————.*Witch Blood! The Diary of a Witch High Priestess*. House of Collectibles, Inc., 1974.

Cuhulain, Kerr. *The Law Enforcement Guide To Wicca*. Horned Owl Publishing, 1997.

Cuhulain, Kerr. *Wiccan Warrior: Walking a Spiritual Path in a Sometimes Hostile World*. Llewellyn Publications, 2000.

Cunningham, Scott. *Cunningham's Encyclopedia of Crystal, Gem, & Metal Magic*. Llewellyn Publications, 1988.

———. *Cunningham's Encyclopedia of Magical Herbs*. Llewellyn Publications, 1985.

Cunningham, Scott, and David Harrington. *The Magical Household: Empower Your Home With Love, Protection, Health, and Happiness*. Llewellyn Publications, 1983.

Cunningham, Scott. *The Truth About Witchcraft Today*. Llewellyn Publications, 1988.

Curott, Phyllis. *Book of Shadows: A Modern Woman's Journey into the Wisdom of Witchcraft and the Magic of the Goddess*. Broadway Books, 1998.

D

Daniélou, Alain. *The Myths and Gods of India: The Classic Work on Hindu Polytheism*. Inner Traditions International, 1985.

Dass, Baba Ram. *Be Here Now*. Lama Foundation, 1971.

Davidson, H. R. Ellis. *Myths and Symbols in Pagan Europe: Early Scandinavian and Celtic Religions*. Syracuse University Press, 1988.

Davidson, Hilda Ellis. *The Lost Beliefs of Northern Europe*. Routledge, 1993.

Day, Brian. *Chronicle of Celtic Folk Customs: A Day-to-Day Guide to Folk Traditions*. Hamlyn, 2000.

De Grandis, Francesca. *Be A Goddess! A Guide to Celtic Spells and Wisdom for Self-Healing, Prosperity, and Great Sex*. Harper San Francisco, 1998.

———. *Goddess Initiation: A Practical Celtic Program for Soul-Healing, Self-Fulfillment and Wild Wisdom*. Harper Collins Publishers, 2001.

Devereux, Paul, John Steele, and David Kubrin. *Earthmind: Tuning in to GAIA Theory with New Age Methods for Saving Our Planet*. Harper & Row, 1989.

Devereux, Paul. *The Illustrated Encyclopedia of Ancient Earth Mysteries*. Cassell & Co., 2000.

Diamond, Irene, and Gloria Feman Orenstein, editors. *Reweaving the World: The Emergence of Ecofeminism*. Sierra Club Books, 1990.

Diamond, Nina L. *Purify Your Body: Natural Remedies for Detoxing from Fifty Everyday Situations*. Crown Paperbacks, 1996.

Dodge, Ellin. *Numerology Has Your Number*. Fireside/Simon & Schuster, 1988.

Domínguez, Ivo, Jr. - Panpipe. *Castings: The Creation of Sacred Space*. Sapfire Productions, Inc., 1996.

Douglas, Nik, and Penny Slinger. *Sexual Secrets: The Alchemy of Ecstasy*. 20th Anniversary Edition, Destiny Books, 2000.

Downing, George, and Anne Kent Rush (illustrator). *The Massage Book*. Random House/Bookworks, 1972.

Drew, A. J. *Wicca Spellcraft for Men: A Spellbook for Male Pagans*. New Page Books, 2001.

Duke, James A., Ph.D. *The Green Pharmacy: New Discoveries in Herbal Remedies for Common Diseases and Conditions from the World's Foremost Authority on Healing Herbs*. Rodale Press, 1997.

E

Edwards, Gill. *Pure Bliss: The Art of Living in Soft Time*. Piatkus, 1999.

Eisler Riane. *The Chalice and the Blade: Our History, Our Future*. Harper Collins, 1987.

————.*Sacred Pleasure: Sex, Myth, and the Politics of the Body— New Paths To Power and Love*. Harper Collins, 1995.

Eliade, Mircea. *Shamanism: Archaic Techniques of Ecstasy*. Princeton University Press, 1964.

Eller, Cynthia. *The Myth of Matriarchal Prehistory: Why an Invented Past Won't Give Women a Future*. Beacon Press, 2000.

Ellerbe, Helen. *The Dark Side of Christian History*. Morningstar and Lark, 1995.

Evans, Arthur. *Witchcraft and the Gay Counterculture: A Radical View of Western Civilization and Some of the People It Has Tried to Destroy*. FAG RAG Books, 1978.

Evans-Wentz, W.Y. *The Fairy-Faith in Celtic Countries*. University Books, 1966.

F

Faraday, Ann, Ph.D. *The Dream Game*. Harper and Row, 1974.

Farrar, Janet and Stewart. *Spells and How They Work*. Robert Hale Limited, 1990.

————. *A Witches' Bible: The Complete Witches' Handbook*. Phoenix Publishing, 1981, 1984,

————. *The Witches' God: Lord of the Dance*. Robert Hale, 1989.

————. *The Witches' Goddess: The Feminine Principle of Divinity*. Robert Hale, 1987.

Farrar, Janet and Stewart, and Gavin Bone. *The Healing Craft: Healing Practices for Witches and Pagans*. Phoenix Publishing, 1999.

Farrar, Stewart. *What Witches Do: The Modern Coven Revealed*. Coward, McCann & Geoghegan, Inc., 1971.

Fitch, Ed. *Magical Rites from the Crystal Well*. Llewellyn Publications, 1984.

Fitch, Eric L. *In Search of Herne the Hunter*. Capall Bann Publishing, 1994.

Flint, Valerie I. J. *The Rise of Magic in Early Medieval Europe*. Princeton University Press, 1991.

Ford, Clyde W. *The Hero With An African Face: Mythic Wisdom of Traditional Africa*. Bantam Books, 1999.

Fortune, Dion. *The Mystical Qabalah*. Samuel Weiser, Inc., 1998.

————. *The Sea Priestess*. Samuel Weiser, Inc., 1957 (originally published 1938).

Fox, Matthew. *Whee! We, Wee All the Way Home... A Guide to the New Sensual Spirituality*. Consortium Books, 1976.

Fox, Selena, et. al., editors. *Circle Guide to Pagan Groups: A Nature Spirituality Networking Sourcebook*. Circle, Annual edition.

Frasier, Debra. *On the Day You Were Born*. Harcourt Brace Jovanovich, Publishers, 1991.

Frazer, Sir James George. *The Golden Bough: A Study in Magic and Religion*. Abridged edition, Macmillan Company, 1951.

Freeman, Mara. *Kindling the Celtic Spirit: Ancient Traditions to Illumine Your Life Throughout the Seasons*. Harper San Francisco, 2001.

G

Gadon, Elinor W. *The Once and Future Goddess: A Sweeping Visual Chronicle of the Sacred Female and Her Reemergence in the Cultural Mythology of Our Time*. Harper & Row, 1989.

Galadriel, Lady. *Magickal and Practical Scented Gifts*. Grove of the Unicorn/Moonstone Publications, 2000.

————. *The Magick of Incenses & Oils*. Grove of the Unicorn/ Moonstone Publications 2001.

————, compiler and editor. *A New Wiccan Book of the Law: A Manual for the Guidance of Groves, Covens, and Individuals*, Second edition. Grove of the Unicorn/Moonstone Publications, 1992.

Gardner, Gerald. *A Goddess Arrives*. I-H-O Books, Reprint Edition 2000 (first published 1939).

————. *The Meaning of Witchcraft*. I-H-O Books, Reprint Edition 2000 (first published 1959)

————. *Witchcraft Today*. I-H-O Books, Reprint Edition 1999 (first published 1954).

————(writing as Scire). *High Magic's Aid*. I-H-O Books, Reprint Edition 1999 (first published 1949).

Gawain, Shakti. *Creative Visualization: Use the Power of Your Imagination to Create What You Want in Life*. Revised edition, New World Library 1995.

George, Demetra. *Mysteries of the Dark Moon: The Healing Power of the Dark Goddess*. Harper Collins, 1992.

George, Leonard, Ph.D. *Alternative Realities: The Paranormal, the Mystic, and the Transcendent in Human Experience*. Facts on File, 1995.

Georges, Robert A., and Michael Owen Jones. *Folkloristics: An Introduction*. Indiana University Press, 1995.

Gillotte, Galen. *Book of Hours: Prayers to the Goddess*. Llewellyn Publications, 2001.

Gimbutas, Marija. *The Civilization of the Goddess: The World of Old Europe*. Harper Collins, 1991.

————. *The Language of the Goddess: Unearthing the Hidden Symbols of Western Civilization*. Harper Collins, 1989.

Ginzburg, Carlo. *Ecstasies: Deciphering the Witches' Sabbath*. Pantheon Books, 1991.

Glass, Justine. *Witchcraft, the Sixth Sense, and Us*. Neville Spearman, 1965.

Goleman, Daniel. *Emotional Intelligence*. Bantam Books, 1994.

Graves, Tom. *The Diviner's Handbook: Your Guide to Divining Anything From Lost Objects, Precious Metals to the Mysteries of Your Own Mind*. Destiny Books, 1986.

Graves, Robert. *The Greek Myths*. Penguin Books, 1960.

————. *The White Goddess: A Historical Grammar of Poetic Myth*. Farrar Straus Giroux, 1948.

Green, Marian. *A Witch Alone: Thirteen Moons to Master Natural Magic*. Aquarian Press, 1991.

Green, Miranda J. *Dictionary of Celtic Myth and Legend*. Thames and Hudson, 1992.

Greer, John Michael. *Inside a Magical Lodge: Group Ritual in the Western Tradition*. Llewellyn Publications, 1998.

Greer, Mary K. *Tarot For Your Self: A Workbook for Personal Transformation*. New Page Books, 1984.

Griffin, Susan. *Woman and Nature: The Roaring Inside Her.* Harper & Row, 1978.

Grimassi, Raven. *Wiccan Magick: Inner Teachings of the Craft.* Llewellyn Publications, 1998.

———. *The Wiccan Mysteries: Ancient Origins & Teachings.* Llewellyn Publications, 1997.

Guiley, Rosemary Ellen. *The Encyclopedia of Witches and Witchcraft.* Facts on File, 1999.

———. *Harper's Encyclopedia of Mystical & Paranormal Experience.* Harper Collins Publishers, 1991.

Gwyn, *Light from the Shadows, A Mythos of Modern Traditional Witchcraft.* Capall Bann Publishing, 1999.

H

Hall, Manly P. *The Secret Teaching of All Ages (An Encyclopedic Outline of Masonic, Hermetic, Qabbalistic and Rosicrucian Symbolical Philosophy, Being an Interpretation of the Secret Teachings concealed within the Rituals, Allegories and Mysteries of All Ages).* Diamond Jubilee Edition, Philosophical Research Society, Inc., 1988.

Harner, Michael. *The Way of the Shaman.* Updated edition, Harper San Francisco, 1990.

Harris, Eleanor and Philip. *The Crafting and Use of Ritual Tools: Step-by-Step Instructions for Woodcrafting Religious and Magical Implements.* Llewellyn Publications, 1998.

Harrow, Judy. *Wicca Covens: How to Start and Organize Your Own.* Citadel Press, 1999.

Harvey, Graham, and Charlotte Hardman. *Paganism Today: Wiccans, Druids, the Goddess and Ancient Earth Traditions for the Twenty-First Century.* Thorsons, 1996.

Hauck, Dennis William. *The Emerald Tablet: Alchemy for Personal Transformation.* Penguin/Arkana, 1999.

Haugk, Kenneth C. *Antagonists in the Church: How to Identify and Deal With Destructive Conflict.* Augsburg Publishing House, 1988.

Hawking, Stephen. *The Illustrated Brief History of Time.* Bantam Books, 1996.

Head, Joseph, and S.L. Cranston, editors. *Reincarnation: The Phoenix Fire Mystery.* Julian Press, 1977.

Heinlein, Robert A. *Stranger in a Strange Land.* G. P. Putnam's Sons, 1961.

Henderson, Julie. *The Lover Within: Opening to Energy in Sexual Practice.* Station Hill/Barrytown, Ltd., 1999.

Hendricks, Gay, Ph.D. *Conscious Breathing: Breathwork for Health, Stress Release, and Personal Mastery*. Bantam Books, 1995.

Heselton, Philip. *Wiccan Roots: Gerald Gardner and the Modern Witchcraft Revival*. Capall Bann Publishing, 2000.

Hipskind, Judith. *Palmistry: the Whole View*. Llewellyn Publications, 1981.

———. *The New Palmistry: How to Read the Whole Hand and Knuckles*. Llewellyn Publications, 1994.

Hofstadter, Douglas R. *Gödel, Escher, Bach: an Eternal Golden Braid, A Metaphorical Fugue on Minds and Machines in the Spirit of Lewis Carroll*. Basic Books, 1999.

Hope, Murry. *Practical Celtic Magic: A Working Guide to the Magical Heritage of the Celtic Races*. The Aquarian Press, 1987.

Hopman, Ellen Evert. *A Druid's Herbal for the Sacred Earth Year*. Destiny Books, 1995.

Hopman, Ellen Evert, and Lawrence Bond. *People of the Earth: The New Pagans Speak Out: Interviews with Margot Adler, Starhawk, Susun Weed, Z. Budapest, and Many Others*. Destiny Books, 1996.

Horne, Fiona. *Witch, A Magickal Journey: A Hip Guide to Modern Witchcraft*. Thorsons, 1998.

Hrisoulas, Jim. *The Complete Bladesmith: Forging Your Way to Perfection*. Paladin Press, 1987.

Hutton, Ronald. *The Stations of the Sun: A History of the Ritual Year in Britain*. Oxford University Press, 1996.

———. *The Triumph of the Moon: A History of Modern Pagan Witchcraft*. Oxford University Press, 1999.

I

Ingerman, Sandra. *Soul Retrieval: Mending the Fragmented Self*. Harper San Francisco, 1991.

J

Jackson, Nigel. *Masks of Misrule: The Horned God and His Cult in Europe*. Capall Bann Publishing, 1996.

Janus-Mithras, Nuit-Hilaria, and Mer-Amun. *Wicca: The Ancient Way*. IllumiNet Press, 1984.

Jeffers, Susan. *Brother Eagle, Sister Sky: A message from Chief Seattle*. Scholastic Inc., 1991.

Johns, June. *King of the Witches: The World of Alex Sanders*. Coward-McCann, 1969.

Johnson, Linda. *Meditation is Boring? Putting Life into Your Spiritual Practice*. Himalayan Institute Press, 2000.

Johnson, Buffie. *Lady of the Beasts: Ancient Images of the Goddess and Her Sacred Animals*. Harper & Row, 1988.

Jones, Diana Wynne. *Charmed Life*. Greenwillow Books, 1977.

———. *The Lives of Christopher Chant*. Greenwillow Books, 1988.

———. *The Magicians of Caprona*. Greenwillow Books, 1980.

———. *Witch Week*. Greenwillow Books, 1982.

Jones, Evan John, with Chas S. Clifton. *Sacred Mask Sacred Dance*. Llewellyn Publications, 1996.

Jones, Prudence, and Caitlín Matthews, editors. *Voices From the Circle: The Heritage of Western Paganism*. Aquarian Press, 1990.

Jones, Prudence, and Nigel Pennick. *A History of Pagan Europe*. Routledge, 1995.

Judith, Anodea. *Wheels of Life: A User's Guide to the Chakra System*. Llewellyn Publications, 1987.

Jung, Carl G. *The Essential Jung: Selected Writings*. Princeton University Press, 1983.

K

K, Amber. *True Magick: A Beginner's Guide*. Llewellyn Publications, 1991.

———. *Covencraft: Witchcraft for Three or More*. Llewellyn Publications, 1998.

Kabat-Zinn, Jon. *Wherever You Go, There You Are: Mindfulness Meditation in Everyday Life*. Hyperion, 1994.

Kaku, Michio. *Hyperspace: A Scientific Odyssey Through Parallel Universes, Time Warps, and the 10th Dimension*. Oxford University Press, 1994.

Kaminski, Patricia, and Richard Katz. *Flower Essence Repertory*. Flower Essence Society, 1994.

Kammen, Carole, & Jodi Gold. *Call to Connection: Bringing Sacred Tribal Values into Modern Life*. Commune-a-Key Publishing, 1998.

Kelly, Aidan A. *Crafting the Art of Magic, Book 1: A History of Modern Witchcraft, 1939-1964*. Llewellyn Publications, 1991.

Kharitidi, Olga, M.D. *Entering the Circle: Ancient Secrets of Siberian Wisdom Discovered by a Russian Psychiatrist*. Harper Collins, 1996.

Kingston, Karen. *Clear Your Clutter With Feng Shui*. Broadway Books, 1998.

Kinsley, David R. *Hindu Goddesses: Visions of the Divine Feminine in the Hindu Religious Tradition*. University of California Press, 1986.

Kinstler, Clysta. *The Moon Under Her Feet*. Harper & Row, 1989.

Kloss, Jethro. *Back to Eden*. Revised and Updated Edition, Lotus Press, 1939/1972.

Knight, Sirona. *Moonflower: Erotic Dreaming with the Goddess*. Llewellyn Publications, 1996.

Knopf, Jim, et al. *Natural Gardening: A Nature Company Guide*. Time Life Books, 1995.

Kondratiev, Alexei. *The Apple Branch: A Path to Celtic Ritual*. The Collins Press, 1998.

Kraig, Donald Michael. *Modern Magick, Eleven Lessons in the High Magical Arts*. Second Edition, Llewellyn Publications, 1998.

Kramer, Heinrich, and James Sprenger. *The Malleus Maleficarum (The Witches' Hammer)*. Dover Publications, 1971.

Kurtz, Katherine, *Lammas Night*. Ballantine Books, 1983.

L

LaChappelle, Dolores. *Sacred Land, Sacred Sex, Rapture of the Deep: Concerning Deep Ecology and Celebrating Life*. Kivakí Press, 1988.

Lamond, Frederic. *Religion Without Beliefs: Essays in Pantheist Theology, Comparative Religion and Ethics*. Janus Publishing Company, 1997.

Lawlor, Robert. *Earth Honoring: the New Male Sexuality*. Park Street Press,1989.

_____. *Sacred Geometry: Philosophy and Practice*. Thames & Hudson, Ltd., 1982.

_____.*Voices of the First Day: Awakening in the Aboriginal Dreamtime*. Inner Traditions International, 1991.

Leach, Maria, editor. *Funk & Wagnall's Standard Dictionary of Folklore, Mythology and Legend*. Funk & Wagnalls, 1972.

Lee, Patrick Jasper. *We Borrow the Earth: An intimate Portrait of the Gypsy Shamanic Tradition and Culture*. Thorsons Publications, 2000.

Leek, Sybil. *The Complete Art of Witchcraft: Penetrating the Mystery Behind Magic Powers*. Leslie Frewin, 1975.

_____. *Diary of a Witch*. Prentice-Hall, Inc., 1968.

Leland, Charles G. *Aradia, or the Gospel of the Witches*. Phoenix Publishing, 1998.

_____.*Etruscan Roman Remains*. Phoenix Publishing, 1999.

Leonard, George. *Mastery: The Keys to Success and Long-Term Fulfillment*. Dutton, 1991.

LeShan, Lawrence. *How to Meditate: A Guide to Self-Discovery*. Little, Brown and Company, 1974.

Leslie, Clare Walker, and Frank E. Gerace. *The Ancient Celtic Festivals: And How We Celebrate Them Today*. Inner Traditions International, 2000.

Lewis, James R., editor. *Magical Religion and Modern Witchcraft*. State University of New York Press, 1996.

Liddell, W.E., and Michael Howard. *The Pickingill Papers: The Origin of the Gardnerian Craft*. Capall Bann Publishing, 1994.

Lorele, Reyna Thera. *The Archer King: Robin of the Wood & the Maid Maerin*. Blue Arrow Books, 1999.

Lorusso, Julia, and Joel Glick. *Healing Stoned: The Therapeutic Use of Gems and Minerals*. Brotherhood of Life, 1976.

Lovelock, J. E. *Gaia: A New Look at Life On Earth*. Oxford University Press, 1979.

M

Mabey, Richard, et. al. *The New Age Herbalist*. Fireside/Simon & Schuster, 1988.

MacKillop, James. *Dictionary of Celtic Mythology*. Oxford University Press, 1998.

MacNeill, Máire. *The Festival of Lughnasa: A Study of the Survival of the Celtic Festival of the Beginning of Harvest*. Oxford University Press, 1962.

Madden, Kristin. *Pagan Parenting: Spiritual, Magical & Emotional Development of the Child*. Llewellyn Publications, 2000.

Maeve Rhea, Lady. *Summoning Forth Wiccan Gods and Goddesses: The Magick of Invocation and Evocation*. Citadel Press, 1999.

Mander, Jerry. *In the Absence of the Sacred: The Failure of Technology and the Survival of the Indian Nations*. Sierra Club Books, 1991.

Mann, Nicholas R. *The Dark God: A Personal Journey Through the Underworld*. Llewellyn Publications, 1996.

Marks, Kate, compiler. *Circle of Song: Songs, Chants, and Dances for Ritual and Celebration*. Full Circle Press, 1993.

Martello, Leo Louis. *Witchcraft: The Old Religion*. University Books, 1973.

Mathers, Samuel Liddell MacGregor, translator. *The Goetia: The Lesser Key of Solomon the King (Clavicula Salomonis Regis)*. Edited with an introduction by Aleister Crowley, illustrated second edition, Samuel Weiser, Inc., 1995.

Matthews, Caitlín. *Celtic Devotional: Daily Prayers and Blessings*. Harmony Books, 1996.

————. *Mabon and the Mysteries of Britain: An Exploration of the Mabinogion*. Arkana, 1987.

Matthews, Caitlín and John. *The Encyclopedia of Celtic Wisdom: A Celtic Shaman's Sourcebook*. Element Books, 1994.

————. *The Western Way: A Practical Guide to the Western Mystery Tradition*. Penguin/Arkana, 1994.

McArthur, Margie. *Wisdom of the Elements: The Sacred Wheel of Earth, Air, Fire, and Water*. Crossing Press, 1998.

McCarley, Becky, and Phil Travers (illustrator). *Herman's Magical Universe*. 1999.

McClure, Susan. *The Herb Gardener: A Guide for All Seasons*. Storey Publishing, 1996.

McColman, Carl. *The Aspiring Mystic: Practical Steps for Spiritual Seekers*. Adams Media Corporation, 2000.

McCoy, Edain. *The Sabbats: A New Approach to Living the Old Ways*. Llewellyn Publications, 1998.

McKenna, Terence. *The Archaic Revival: Speculations on Psychedelic Mushrooms, the Amazon, VIrtual Reality, UFOs, Evolution, Shamanism, the Rebirth of the Goddess, and the End of History*. Harper Collins, 1991.

McLelland, Lilith. *Spellcraft: A Primer for the Young Magician*. Eschaton Productions, Inc., 1997.

McMahon, Joanne D. S., Ph.D., and Anna M. Lascurain, Esq. *Shopping For Miracles: A Guide to Psychics & Psychic Powers*. Lowell House, 1997.

McNeill, F. Marian. *The Silver Bough, Volume One: Scottish Folklore and Folk-Belief*. William MacLellan, 1957.

————. *The Silver Bough, Volume Two: A Calendar of Scottish National Festivals: Candlemas to Harvest Home*. William MacLellan, 1959.

————. *The Silver Bough, Volume Three: A Calendar of Scottish National Festivals: Hallowe'en to Yule*. Stuart Titles Ltd., 1961.

————. *The Silver Bough, Volume Four: The Local Festivals of Scotland*. Stuart Titles Ltd., 1968.

McWhorter, Margaret Lange. *Tea Cup Tales: The Art of Tea Leaf Reading*. Ransom Hill Press, 1998.

Melody, *Love is in the Earth: A Kaleidoscope of Crystals*, Updated edition. Earth-Love Publishing House, 1995.

Merivale, Patricia. *Pan the Goat-God: His Myth in Modern Times*. Harvard University Press, 1969.

Merrifield, Ralph. *The Archaeology of Ritual and Magic*. Guild Publishing, 1987.

Meyer, Marvin W., editor. *The Ancient Mysteries: A Sourcebook of Sacred Texts*. University of Pennsylvania Press, 1987.

Middleton, Julie Forest, editor and compiler. *Songs for Earthlings: A Green Spirituality Songbook*. Emerald Earth Publishing, 1998.

Miller, Hamish, and Paul Broadhurst. *The Sun and the Serpent: An Investigation into Earth Energies*. Pendragon Press, 1989.

Miller, Timothy, Ph.D. *How to Want What You Have: Discovering the Magic and Grandeur of Ordinary Existence*. Henry Holt and Company, 1995.

Mindell, Arnold. *Sitting in the Fire: Large Group Transformation Using Conflict and Diversity*. Lao Tse Press, 1995.

Mitchison, Naomi. *The Corn King and the Spring Queen*. Overlook Press, 1990 (originally published 1931).

Monroe, Robert A. *Journeys Out of the Body: The Classic Work on Out-of-Body Experience*. Main Street Books/Doubleday, 1971.

Moorey, Teresa and Howard. *Pagan Gods for Today's Man: A Beginner's Guide*. Hodder & Stoughton, 1997.

Mountainwater, Shekhinah. *Ariadne's Thread: A Workbook of Goddess Magic*. The Crossing Press, 1991.

Murray, Margaret. *The God of the Witches*. Oxford University Press, 1952.

———. *The Witch-Cult in Western Europe*. Oxford University Press, 1921.

N

Neihardt, John G. *Black Elk Speaks: Being the Life Story of a Holy Man of the Oglala Sioux*. University of Nebraska Press, 1932.

Nicholson, Shirley, and Brenda Rosen, compilers. *Gaia's Hidden Life: The Unseen Intelligence of Nature*. Quest Books, 1992.

Niman, Michael I. *People of the Rainbow: A Nomadic Utopia*. University of Tennessee Press, 1997.

O

Ó hÓgáin, Dáithí. *Myth, Legend & Romance: An Encyclopedia of the Irish Folk Tradition*. Prentice Hall Press, 1991.

———. *The Sacred Isle: Belief and Religion in Pre-Christian Ireland*. The Boydell Press, 1999.

O'Donohue, John. *Anam Cara: A Book of Celtic Wisdom*. Cliff Street Books/Harper Collins, 1997.

O'Gaea, Ashleen. *The Family Wicca Book: The Craft for Parents and Children*. Llewellyn Publications, 1998.

Orion, Loretta. *Never Again the Burning Times: Paganism Revived*. Waveland Press, 1995.

Orman, Suze. *The 9 Steps to Financial Freedom: Practical & Spiritual Steps So You Can Stop Worrying.* Crown Publishers, Inc., 1997.

Orr, Emma Restall. *Spirits of the Sacred Grove: The World of a Druid Priestess.* Thorsons, 1998.

Osborn, Kevin, and Dana L. Burgess, Ph.D. *The Complete Idiot's Guide to Classical Mythology.* Alpha Books, 1998.

P

Parrinder, Geoffrey. *Mysticism in the World's Religions.* Oneworld Publications, 1976.

Patai, Raphael. *The Hebrew Goddess,* Third enlarged edition. Wayne State University Press, 1990.

Paterson, Jacqueline Memory. *Tree Wisdom: The Definitive Guidebook to the Myth, Folklore and Healing Power of Trees.* Thorsons, 1996.

Pauwels, Louis, and Jacques Bergier. *The Morning of the Magicians.* Dorset Press, 1963.

Pearson, Joanne, Richard H. Roberts, and Geoffrey Samuels, editors. *Nature Religion Today: Paganism in the Modern World.* Edinburgh University Press, 1998.

Pennick, Nigel. *Celtic Sacred Landscapes.* Thames and Hudson, 1996.

————. *Crossing the Borderlines: Guising, Masking & Ritual Animal Disguises in the European Tradition.* Capall Bann Publishing, 1998.

————. *Magical Alphabets.* Samuel Weiser, Inc., 1992

————. *The Pagan Book of Days: A Guide to the Festivals, Traditions, and Sacred Days of the Year.* Destiny Books, 2001.

Pepper, Elizabeth, and John Wilcock, editors. *The Witches' Almanac.* The Witches' Almanac, Ltd., annual edition.

Perkins, John. *Shape Shifting: Shamanic Techniques for Global and Personal Transformation.* Destiny Books, 1997.

————.*The World is as You Dream It: Shamanic Teachings From the Amazon and Andes.* Destiny Books, 1994.

Pickands, Marcia L. *Psychic Abilities: How to Train and Use Them.* Samuel Weiser, Inc., 1999.

Plourde, Lynn, and Greg Couch (illustrator). *Wild Child.* Simon and Schuster, 1999.

Pollack, Rachel. *The Body of the Goddess: Sacred Wisdom in Myth, Landscape, and Culture.* Element Books, 1997.

————. *Seventy-Eight Degrees of Wisdom: A Book of Tarot.* 1997

Pratchett, Terry. *Wyrd Sisters.* ROC/Penguin, 1988.

Puhvel, Jaan. *Comparative Mythology.* Johns Hopkins University Press, 1987.

R

RavenWolf, Silver. *Halloween: Customs, Recipes & Spells*. Llewellyn Publications, 1999.

Redmond, Layne. *When the Drummers Were Women: A Spiritual History of Rhythm*. Three Rivers Press, 1997.

Reed, Ellen Cannon. *The Heart of Wicca: Wise Words from a Crone on the Path*. Samuel Weiser, Inc., 2000.

―――. *The Witches Qabala: The Pagan Path and the Tree of Life*. Samuel Weiser, Inc., 1997.

―――. *The Witches Tarot*. Llewellyn Publications, 1989.

Rees, Alwyn and Brinley. *Celtic Heritage: Ancient Tradition in Ireland and Wales*. Grove Press, Inc., 1961.

Regardie, Israel. *The Complete Golden Dawn System of Magic*. New Falcon Publications, 1990.

Reid, Lori. *Moon Magic: How to Use the Moon's Phases to Inspire and Influence Your Relationships, Home Life and Business*. Three Rivers Press, 1998.

Reif, Jennifer. *Mysteries of Demeter: Rebirth of the Pagan Way*. Samuel Weiser, Inc., 1999.

Richardson, Alan. *Earth God Rising: The Return of the Male Mysteries*. Llewellyn Publications, 1992.

Rico, Gabriele Lusser. *Writing the Natural Way: Using Right-Brain Techniques to Release Your Expressive Powers*. Tarcher/Putnam, 1983.

Robbins, Tom. *Jitterbug Perfume*. Bantam Books, 1984.

Roberts, Elizabeth, and Elias Amidon, editors. *Earth Prayers From Around the World: 365 Prayers, Poems, and Invocations for Honoring the Earth*. Harper Collins, 1991.

Robertson, Laurel, Carol Flinders, and Brian Ruppenthal, *The New Laurel's Kitchen: A Handbook for Vegetarian Cookery & Nutrition*. Ten Speed Press. 1986.

Ross, Anne. *Pagan Celtic Britain: Studies in Iconography and Tradition*. Academy Chicago Publishers, 1996 (reprint of 1967 edition).

Roszak, Theodore, Mary E. Gomes, and Allen D. Kanner, editors. *Ecopsychology: Restoring the Earth, Healing the Mind*. Sierra Club Books, 1995.

Roth, Gabrielle, with John Loudon. *Maps to Ecstasy: A Healing Journey for the Untamed Spirit*. New World Library, 1998.

Roth, Gabrielle. *Sweat Your Prayers: Movement as Spiritual Practice*. Tarcher/Putnam, 1997.